# Old Testament History

Life and Religion Series

# Old Testament History

By

## Frank Knight Sanders, Ph.D., D.D.

Sometime Woolsey Professor of Biblical Literature
in Yale University

Director of the Board of Missionary Preparation

Edited by

## Frank K. Sanders
&
## Henry A. Sherman

**Ross & Perry, Inc.**
Washington, D.C.

Ross & Perry, Inc. Publishers
216 G St., N.E.
Washington, D.C. 20002
Telephone (202) 675-8300
Facsimile (202) 675-8400
info@RossPerry.com

SAN 253-8555

Library of Congress Control Number: 2002107533
http://www.rossperry.com

ISBN 1-932080-94-5

Book Cover designed by Sapna. sapna@rossperry.com

♻ The paper used in this publication meets the requirements for permanence
established by the American National Standard for Information Sciences
"Permanence of Paper for Printed Library Materials" (ANSI Z39.48-1984).

# PREFACE

This volume, like the other volumes of the series, aims to furnish to the untechnically trained reader or student a succinct yet trustworthy and satisfying introduction to the subject of which it treats. It will lay a foundation on which can be reared an illuminating, constructive understanding of the Old Testament as a whole. A well-balanced knowledge of the history found in the Old Testament is quite essential to this larger comprehension. Such knowledge need not be in close detail but must be well organized.

This volume makes four specific contributions which will repay the careful reader or student. Its analytical outline of the history by chapters will enable one to carry the whole history in mind as a unity. Again, its assembling, section by section, of all of the actual historical material discussed brings the student face to face with the facts with which he deals. Moreover, its emphasis on essentials brings into relief the data which every thoughtful student of the Bible ought to know and indicates their value estimated from the standpoints of history, religion, ethics, and life. Finally, its brief compass encourages the student to actually achieve the ability to survey the whole Old Testament in a historical perspective which is sane, balanced, and adequate for all foundational needs. His task thereafter will be the filling in of details.

No space is given in this series to argument over technical details. For these the student must go to larger volumes, to which ample references are given in the appendices. The desire has been to make a readable volume, yet suited, in connection with *Old Testament Prophecy*, for use as a text-book for college classes aiming at a rapid survey of the Old Testament, for Bible classes, for teacher-training classes in community schools of religion and elsewhere, and furnishing the essential data for profitable discussion.

The Appendix furnishes apparatus for the aid of the teacher or class leader. Every reader can test his grasp of Old Testament history by answering the questions in the fourth section of the Appendix. For classroom discussions the suggested topics in Appendix V will be found useful. No questions are raised that cannot reasonably be discussed by those using this book. The first four volumes of the series of which this is a part give a correct perspective for both the Old and the New Testament. Each volume, however, is complete in itself.

No one should expect that the study of so small a volume will afford a mastery of Old Testament history. The book has a less pretentious but more useful aim. It will lay a secure basis for an appreciation of the dignity, interest, and value of Old Testament history, for its intelligent interpretation, and for a lifelong enjoyment of the Old Testament as a whole.

THE EDITORS.

# CONTENTS

# CONTENTS

# OLD TESTAMENT HISTORY

# OLD TESTAMENT HISTORY

## INTRODUCTION

A comprehensive knowledge of the historical material of the Old Testament is of real value to all who teach any portion of the Bible or who give religious instruction. The Old Testament records the religious growth of the Hebrew people from a stage of very simple religious development until they became fitted to be instrumental in conveying to humankind sound religious impressions regarding God, man, and the universe. God made use of other peoples and even of other religious achievements, but the predominantly significant historical religious movement, which opened the way for the best religious life of to-day, came to the world by way of the Hebrew people and was given an adequate record in the Old Testament.

This historical development ought to be clearly understood by every student of religion, whether in the pulpit, in the school of religion, or on the mission field, at home or abroad. It is fundamental to an understanding of the whole revelation of God to mankind. That revelation was an historical process, centuries in length, its progress slow at some periods, exceedingly rapid at other times. Students of the Old Testament should have a real grasp of the whole course of this progress. Many never see it in its proper balance and with a true perspective. Of the twelve or more centuries of Hebrew and Jewish history from the days of Moses down to the birth of Jesus Christ, four were con-

1

sumed by the Hebrew people in getting ready to make
real history; during the next four a climax of religious
culture was reached; the last four centuries counted
for conservatism rather than for advance.   Manifestly,
the four centuries following 800 B. C. should be those
most carefully explored and interpreted.   As a matter
of fact these centuries are rarely, except by special students, given their proper proportion of attention.   This
volume seeks to show their creative contributions.

A student of religious subjects needs more than a
mere knowledge of Old Testament data.   It is desirable that, unassisted in any way whatsoever, he should
gain the ability to think at will through the events of
these important centuries; to rate at its true relative
value each stage of the political, social, and religious
progress which they embody; and to visualize each
stage or period as a complete unit with its great leaders, its significant events, its religious thinking, and its
outstanding contribution to the historical process of
upward growth.   The Old Testament thus becomes a
real possession at the command of the student or
teacher.   The interpretation of any portion is regulated and illumined by the comprehensive knowledge
of the whole range of development.   Such knowledge
will become wholly satisfying only after prolonged
study, since the Old Testament is a library of history
and literature rather than one single book, yet the
process can be begun rightly, and, thus begun, will
richly reward the student from the very beginning.

The rapid study outlined in this volume will enable
a student to lay the proper foundation for a right beginning.   The one who seeks a mastery of the whole
Bible and of the Bible as a whole must pay the necessary price.   Such a grasp will not be the outcome of
one winter's study, but of that of years.   The process

is more than the adding of fresh data to those already known. It involves the constant realignment of one's whole body of knowledge regarding the Scriptures in accordance with each group of freshly gathered data.

One very definite religious advantage is gained by the careful, persistent study of Old Testament History and Literature. It is the gradual organization and enrichment of personal religious experience. The very lines of teaching and experience which matured that nation's thoughtful leaders bring maturity and a sense of responsibility and relationship to the Divine to young and old to-day. A thoughtful study of the Old Testament is in itself a course of religious training. This course is all the more valuable because the final expression or at least the most satisfying expression of matured religious experience was given by Jesus Christ. The revelation that preceded his day was at best a helpful introduction to the perfect revelation to which he gave expression of the Divine in relationship with humanity, of the rich possibilities of human religious experience and of a true philosophy of the world of sentient life. Yet one who has trodden the historical pathway which led up to the Christian era is far better prepared to appreciate Christ's outlook over life.

The plan of this volume, as of the others in this series, magnifies the actual Biblical material at the expense of interpretation. By the outlines printed in smaller type the student is enabled to traverse for himself the whole range of Biblical history in historical sequence. The comments are purposely restricted to such as clarify and organize the historical facts.

The limitations of this volume forbid the discussion of each distinct era in Hebrew history by itself. An outline of the history which aims to do full justice to each period will be found in the appendix.

# I

## PRE–MOSAIC BEGINNINGS OF HEBREW HISTORY

GENESIS 1–50 (BEFORE 1200 B. C.)

The Book of Genesis is a book of beginnings. It covers an indefinite range of centuries from the dawn of life to the days of Moses. It is an extraordinary book. It has some of the qualities of a drama; frequently it seems as personal as a biography; it deals epically with a great sweep of history; it includes many data which seem whimsical and petty. As a unit, however, Genesis furnishes in three ways a strong introduction to the biblical story of the centuries of expanding Hebrew life. It presents the origins of the Hebrews as a people, chosen in some sense to do their part in the world's growth. It reveals deep qualities of character as the justification of that choice. It expresses the broad, sound, basal religious convictions which differentiated them from their neighboring and related peoples, and made them useful channels of God's revelation of Himself to the world.

A discriminating reader quickly realizes that Genesis is no such balanced, smoothly moving, historical narrative as I Samuel. Charming narratives alternate with mere catalogues of names. It is a treasure-house of richly varied material, hard to unify. It is, nevertheless, as a whole a moving survey, covering many centuries, which traces the gradual emergence of the

4

Hebrews into the realm of history as a people for whom God had marked out a noble destiny.

Such surveys are not made on the spot. They are interpretations of ages that have passed away. The Genesis we read is a book with a long literary history. It was based upon at least three earlier Hebrew writings, each noble in quality and reverent in purpose. One of these, by a writer of prophetic temperament, aimed to show God's share in the origin, the early history, and the growth of the Hebrew race. From this book came the bulk of the direct historical narrative in Genesis. Another, written also by a man of prophetic mind and probably at a little later date, sought to commemorate the great leadership of the early eras and to indicate the sacred spots where these men of God had had unforgetable experiences of the Divine. This book was the chief source of the remarkable portraitures in Genesis. The third was probably written by one of priestly training, who believed that religion and its institutions were the most important heritage of his people from that distant past. His narrative furnished the greater part of the impressive religious setting of Genesis. The author of Genesis, a man of comprehensive understanding, sought to combine into one narrative the tested values of each of these helpful narratives. His method seems to have been that of compilation. As far as possible he made literal extracts from these earlier writings, altering or adjusting only so far as was necessary to make a readable narrative. That he adopted this method is a cause for devout thankfulness. The student of to-day can be assured that Genesis represents the divine illumining of four great souls instead of one, and can rejoice that it is the precious deposit of centuries of religious interpretation and growth. The fact that Genesis is a compilation explains adequately the surprising turns of style, viewpoint, and religious experience, encountered not only in the first two or three chapters, but repeatedly. Genesis records the events of centuries but reflects the ideas of many more.

The fifty chapters of Genesis cover the history of the world, as these writers knew it, down to the thirteenth century B. C. Their available data were the perplexing, crudely historical traditions which are all that remain from the primitive days of any race. These data represented to the writers a distant past. They were interpreted with real insight and with loving appreciation to show through the legends of racial beginnings and through local traditions and tribal memoranda the stirrings of a great God-given impulse toward a new type of national life. The call of a people by God to achieve what no other people could do so well was the golden thread by means of which the writers of Genesis found their way out of the mysteries of primitive history. This idea caused its author to personalize the narrative, giving it human values and vividness, and making it permanently useful. Instead of telling the story of these centuries by periods, he related it by patriarchs. It is not the story of the third millennium B. C., but that of Abraham, Jacob, and Joseph. Thus Genesis became something infinitely greater than an accurate tradition. It is a real Bible, a writing which drives home the conviction that God is in His world and that history exhibits the gradual outworking of His plans.

1. **The Narratives of Human Beginnings (Genesis 1–11).**

The first eleven chapters of Genesis embody the ideas which were held by the Hebrew people about the beginnings of human history. Up to the middle of the nineteenth century or even later, all reverent students of Scripture held that, because these declarations were found in the Bible, they must be upheld to the least detail as having divine authority. The past half century has conferred three inestimable boons upon a Bible-loving, reverent Christianity seeking a truer interpretation of Scripture. It has, in the first place, caused the general acceptance of the sciences of geology, ethnology, archæology, and the like as being on the whole trustworthy interpreters of the many unsolved mysteries of the beginnings of the universe. For light on these origins, human or otherwise, we turn to them. Again, it has brought to light the rich earlier heritage of the Hebrews as a race. The astonishingly rich and instructive results of archæological and linguistic researches in the Assyro-Babylonian and Syria-Palestinian regions and in Egypt have shown beyond contention that the Hebrew stories of Genesis are essentially one with a larger body of older traditions. The declarations of Genesis 1-11 are paralleled with curious accuracy and increasing completeness by those of the literatures so long buried. But the third and greatest advantage to the Christian interpreter of Genesis conferred by the past half century has been due to a close comparison between these early traditions as found in Babylonian literature and the same traditions as given in Genesis. While a kinship is manifest, they seem transformed from stories which are more or less ridiculous into stories which are sublime. This transformation was exactly what made the difference between a mere traditional story of a world coming into being under the conflicting will of many gods and the sublime account of its orderly creation by one divine Mind, or of a deluge brought on by jealousies among the gods and a deluge through which God gave a corrupted world a fresh ethical start.  The Hebrew writers used the traditional material to serve as a convenient, familiar vehicle for a series of declarations of fundamental religious importance.  These religious ideas are those for which the reader should look.  They go to the very heart of human religious experience.  They make these chapters a suitable and adequate introduction to the whole course of history which the Bible unfolds.

The true God revealed in His work of creation.   Genesis 1 : 1–2 : 4a.
The Divine provisions for man's perfect development.   2 : 4b–25.
Man's deliberate disobedience of the divine commands and the
tragic consequences.   3 : 1–24.
Cain, his brother's murderer, sentenced to be a perpetual wanderer.
4 : 1–16.
His descendants, those of Seth and the ten antediluvians.   4 : 17–
5 : 32.
The flood God's radical cure for persistent sinfulness: its preva-
lence, the preservation of a righteous group, the new covenant
of promise for mankind.   6 : 1–9 : 17.
Noah's blessing of Shem, the forefather of all Semitic peoples.
9 : 18–28.
The nations of the Hebrew world and their relationships.   10.
How different languages came to be spoken.   11 : 1–9.
The genealogical line from Shem to Abraham.   11 : 10–26.

Two great motives of the author of Genesis are clearly revealed by a careful study of these chapters, the desire to exhibit the direct descent from the first human being to Abraham, and the desire to show the adequate religious foundations of the history to be related.  The important element of these narratives does not lie in the facts which they relate.  There is no real value in determining the geological accuracy of the stately poem which describes God's work of creation.  It is even less important to locate the garden of Eden or to dis-cover whether a vessel of the dimensions of the Ark could hold every known species of beast.  Nor is it supremely important for the average student to distinguish accurately each strand of original narrative in Genesis. The heart of these chapters is the true religious idealism which the writer expressed through these ancient stories. What he really aimed to set forth was the sovereignty of God in His world, His gracious purposes and His goodness, His watchful attitude toward the world He has made, man's unique likeness to God, his dominant place in God's universe, his moral responsibility, the sure consequences of sinfulness, the never-ending struggle with evil, God's share in promoting the survival of the morally fit in the world, His constant affording of opportunity for righteous progress, the brotherhood of humankind, and God's active share in world progress. These are great ideas. They make history not merely intelligible but inspiring. One who reviews them can see how wonderfully Genesis 1–11 introduces the Biblical story.

## 2. The World as It Was About 2000 B. C.

The end of the third millennium before Christ was a turning-point in world history. It marked the beginnings of history as we are accustomed to measure it. At about that date Babylonian civilization, profiting by a thousand years of slow but steady cultural advance, was imperially organized and established by the famous Hammurabi. At about the same time, in the Nile valley, the Egyptian civilization of the feudal age reached its peak of prosperity. These two genuinely cultured nations dominated the world of that day.

It was not a large world as compared with ours, hardly greater than the Turkish empire of half a century ago. Much of it was desert or mountainous. The portion that counted most constituted a "fertile crescent" with the Nile valley at one extreme and the

Tigris-Euphrates valley at the other. What we know as Palestine, Syria, and Mesopotamia lay between these two centres of civilization, Asia Minor being a sort of "hinterland." Settled groups of Canaanites[1] inhabited Palestine; the Phœnicians held the coast; the Amorite clans inhabited Syria; the Hittites were becoming formidable in Asia Minor; and the Assyrians were a rapidly developing people on the upper Tigris. Over the habitable desert roamed many independent tribes.

It was a rapidly changing world. Its law was force. Those who had vigor and enterprise but no wealth looked covetously upon the resources of the peoples of the settled parts. Great changes of environment were often taking place. Organization and growth were the price of continuing existence anywhere. Peoples were consciously in the making. Leadership had its utmost opportunity.

It was a world whose variety and accessibility gave promise of a strong future. Within it were the heirs of a stable civilization already ancient and many-sided. Within it also were restless, roaming peoples of very primitive culture. Along the whole length of the crescent was a stream of interchange and activity. The opportunity was thus afforded for the rapid development of a yet higher civilization.

### 3. The Gradual Development of a Hebrew People.

Genesis 12–50 tells the story of the emergence of the Hebrew clans into the light of history. In the closing chapters the reigning Pharaoh assigns lands within his Egyptian domains to them. From Egypt they were delivered in the twelfth century B. C. The length of

[1] Canaanites and Amorites were probably the same people, at least very closely akin.

their stay in Egypt and their earlier history are matters which are quite obscure.

᾿ Genesis seems at first sight to relate the early history in a very simple and clear fashion, declaring that the Hebrews were the descendants of Jacob who was the grandson of Abraham, who was the single ancestor of all. But such a statement overlooks many of the data which these chapters furnish, and many others which archæological research has brought to light. It seems clear, however, that the Hebrews were of desert stock, that they, as known in later history, developed out of several groups of tribes, only one of which was surely in Egypt, and that the exact movements of these groups cannot be traced with assurance in the varied records of Genesis. These conclusions being accepted, it is equally true that the most important and directive section of the Hebrews did find its way to Egypt, there to undergo varied experiences.

It is clear that the Hebrews as a race were children of the desert. Probably they were a part of that great migration of desert peoples into the more habitable and fertile regions of western Asia which took place in the middle centuries of the second millennium before Christ. They recognized a direct kinship with the Aramæan peoples; they also claimed Babylonian descent. The exact proportions of their ancestral blood it is impossible now to determine. Of more importance is the implied claim that the Hebrew heritage was of the best. A desert-bred people may have choice leadership.

This desert heritage accounted for three important facts which need to be understood as underlying all Hebrew beginnings. When first appearing in history as a recognized human group, the Hebrews were nomads, wandering folk, dwellers in tents, loving broad acres.

They were at this time organized by clans or families, each very independent, the clan, not the individual, being their unit of society. Their religious life was very simple. Exodus 6 : 3 recognizes this fact. Their religious life, like that of all nomads, resembled that of a child; it was imaginative, simple, direct, unreflective.

We may be very grateful that the prophetic historians put the traditions of these formative centuries into a form so strongly personalized. The patriarchs may have been idealized even to a large extent, but, even so, the resultant portraitures reflected the historic ideals of the race. Through the loving pen of the patriot we reach sound ideals of racial character and purpose. Abraham, Jacob, and Joseph embody in rich detail the qualities which gave the Hebrews a working place in God's world. As personalities they are richly deserving of study.

### 4. The Stories Relating to Abraham (Genesis 11 : 27–25 : 18).

These chapters contain a series of fascinating narratives about Abraham and his people. They are so straightforward and vivid as to make the reader forget that they describe the origins of a race. They portray a great character.

> The migration of Abraham, the Semite, to Canaan. Genesis 11 : 27–12 : 9.
> His great-heartedness in dealing with Lot, his kinsman. 13 : 1–18.
> His prowess and dignity. 14.
> His covenants with God. 15, 17.
> The strengthening of Abraham's faith in God's justice. 18; 19 : 1–14, 24–28.
> How Abraham met the supreme test of loyalty to God. 21 : 1–8; 22 : 1–19.
> His purchase of a burial place. 23.
> The finding of Rebekah for his son Isaac. 24.
> The other lines of descent from Abraham. 16; 21 : 9–21; 25 :1–18.

The accuracy with which these narratives portray a desert chieftain of the highest class and his customs is almost uncanny. They likewise depict a great personality, large-minded, far-seeing, clothed with responsibility, hospitable, self-respecting, courageous, unselfish, courteous, truly devoted to God. Abraham's character stood all reasonable tests. He was a man of his age, not of ours; but he lived a life in fellowship with the Unseen. He had the qualities of a great pioneer, for he ventured forth for a principle and withheld nothing. His portraiture is an impressive sermon to any age.

The quality of these narratives is remarkable. The stories of Abraham's departure (12 : 1–8), of his dealings with Lot (13 : 1–18), of the blood covenant with God (15 : 1–20), of the visit of the angels (18), of the sacrifice of Isaac (22 : 1–19), of the bargaining with the Hittites (23), and of the wooing of Rebekah (24) are inimitable sketches. They are masterpieces of literature, while being at the same time a reservoir of social and religious data of the first importance.

5. **The Stories Which Centre About Jacob (25 : 19–35 : 29).**

These narratives seem to trace the origin of the whole Hebrew commonwealth to Jacob as one ancestor, counting each tribe as having descended from one of his sons. But the Bible itself furnishes evidence that the Hebrew people, as known in history, were a mixed race, growing by adoption as well as by natural descent. The exact reconciliation of these apparently opposite facts may never be possible. It has been conjectured that the adopted tribes were those described as the descendants of concubine mothers. Whatever the real historical explanation of the origin of all Israel may be, there can be no doubt that there was an ancestor, Jacob, from whom all the Hebrews of later centuries took pride in tracing their descent, that of his unquestioned descendants a representative section found their way eventually to Egypt, and that these inimitable narratives about him embody a series of studies in character transformation, which are priceless. Their picture of patriarchal nomadic conditions, of the steady increase in prosperity and importance of the tribesmen, and of an eventual transfer to Egypt because of famine is wholly in accordance with probable fact. The essential value of the narratives lies, however, in their life-like studies of moral growth.

> The two sons of Isaac and Rebekah: Esau, the rude, thoughtless hunter; Jacob, the gentle, crafty, but far-sighted home-dweller. Genesis 25: 19–34.
> How Rebekah and Jacob obtained for Jacob by fraud the patriarchal blessing and the outcome.   27: 1–45.
> Jacob's vision of God at Bethel and his vow of faithful service. 28: 1–5, 10–22.
> How Jacob married Leah and Rachel in Haran and became wealthy by matching his cunning against that of their father.   29: 1–30: 43.
> His eager return to Canaan, his homeland, having made a covenant of peace with Laban, his father-in-law.   31: 1–55.
> His scheme for satisfying Esau's revengefulness.   32: 3–21; 33.
> His moral transformation at the Jabbok.   32: 22–32.
> The new Jacob in whose heart religion became a great reality.   35.

It is interesting to note the distinctiveness of these loving yet faithful portraits. The great-hearted Abraham with his unselfishness, courage, and faith was no more in fellowship with the Unseen than Jacob, the crafty and unscrupulous, yet wise and persevering, came to be. The generous but shallow Esau, the scheming and masterful Rebekah, the greedy Laban, like the small-minded Lot, are to be studied as sermons in biography. Each characterization carries its own moral. So does the history of Jacob. He paid well for his craftiness.

## 6. The Stories Which Centre About Joseph (37–50).

These beautiful narratives, so full of charm, are likewise full of moral idealism. They uphold sturdy conceptions of integrity, trustworthiness, sincerity, and faith. The fact that the early patriarchal traditions took such a form instead of mere tales of prowess is a first-rate proof of the innate idealism of the Hebrew mind. Historically they tell the story of the transfer of a large portion, at least, of the Hebrew clans to Egypt, where Hebrew history really began.

Joseph, Jacob's favorite son, sold by his brothers into Egyptian slavery. Genesis 37.
How he came, through his faithfulness and ability, to be appointed governor of Egypt by the Pharaoh. 38–41.
His forgiving welcome of his famine-stricken family. 42 : 1–45 : 26.
The last days of Jacob and of Joseph in Egypt. 45 : 27–50 : 26.

Thus the tribesmen who had lived a free life for generations in the desert were settled on the border of Egypt under the control of the sovereign of that great empire. The immediate cause was a famine. The author of Genesis sought to show that it was really a step in the fulfilment of God's abiding purpose for the world, none the less important because no one realized its significance at the time.

The keenest criticism ever made regarding these chapters was based upon their excellence. It has been declared that Joseph is too perfect a personality. His portrait is indeed ideal. Joseph was the true child of the godly Jacob. But the repentant Judah is a noble personality. One of the most moving passages in the Old Testament is his intercession for Benjamin (44 :

18–34).  Moreover, Jacob's own portrait is completed in his interview with the Pharaoh (47 : 7–10).

## 7.  The Elements of Abiding Value in Genesis.

One who surveys Genesis as a whole realizes the unique and commanding value of the book as it stands, and never fails to marvel over the genius it exhibits. How fortunate it has been for the religious world that the merely historical data of these centuries are obscured in the portrayal of personalities.  No writer of early Hebrew days could possibly have related the correct historical data.  No one is sure of them even to-day after nearly a century of research concerning the early ages.  Yet Genesis is an unsurpassable introduction to the Biblical story of the growth of the Hebrew people into religious leadership.  The foundation it lays is ethical and spiritual.  It drives home the impression of a world made gradually ready for righteous living and the equally gradual appearance of a people who would interpret godliness to the world.  It makes this impression through a series of pictures flashed upon a background which is not clearly defined.  The Hebrews are yet in the simplest stage of social and religious organization.  They have their whole career yet to be achieved.

# II

## THE FORMATIVE INFLUENCE OF THE
## GREAT LEADER, MOSES

Exodus, Leviticus, Numbers, and Deuteronomy
(About 1200–1150 B. C.)

With the settlement of an important section of the
Hebrew tribes in Egypt a new era began for them
and for the world. This was not due to environment
merely; quite possibly the stay in Egypt did little for
the Hebrews as a group, since their own habits and
preferences made for seclusion. It doubtless had more
effect on their natural leaders. Moses may not have
been the only promising Hebrew lad who was introduced to the culture of the Egypt of that day. The
Hebrews in any case maintained their identity as a
people and were not merged into the Egyptian nation.

1. **The Chronology.**

To determine the exact dates of their entrance into
Egypt or of their great departure is impracticable.
All early Biblical chronology is uncertain. Events,
however important, earlier than about the ninth century B. C. must be dated provisionally, with much
allowance for variation. They can only be approxi-
mated. Many Biblical estimates are in round numbers. No one can be sure, for example, that Moses
lived exactly one hundred and twenty years (Deuteronomy 34 : 7), although he must have become very old.

17

The Biblical statements about the sojourn of the Hebrews in Egypt point on the one hand to four centuries (Genesis 15 : 13; Exodus 12 : 40), and on the other to four generations (Genesis 15 : 15; Exodus 6 : 16–20). The shorter estimate seems on the whole the more probable. Its terminus and hence the time of the active career of Moses would be approximately determined, if we knew without question who was the Egyptian sovereign "who knew not Joseph." From such hints as are available he is usually identified with Ramses II, the greatest sovereign of the nineteenth dynasty.

## 2. The Egypt Which the Hebrews Knew.

The Egypt which made the background for the Hebrew story was the Egypt of the Empire which lasted from about 1580 to 1150 B. C. About this there can be little question. Its Pharaohs were great military leaders who conquered a vast empire which extended from the upper Euphrates to Ethiopia. The wealth thus captured developed the splendid Egypt, whose ruins even to-day are so impressive. Art, architecture, and literature flourished under the patronage of the great Pharaohs whose capital was at Thebes. Most of the massive monumental remains now visible date from this remarkable era.

In such a rapidly growing empire the time was bound to come when the friendly conditions under which the Hebrews gained entrance into Egypt would be forgotten or deliberately foresworn and they would be forced, like other foreigners, to toil upon the imposing exhibits of royal ambition or enterprise.

During several of these same centuries a Hittite empire developed in Asia Minor (about 1450–1200 B. C.), which was powerful enough to dispute with Egypt the

suzerainty of the smaller peoples of Syria and Palestine. The Tel-el Amarna correspondence between the
Egyptian sovereign and his representatives abroad,
written in the latter part of the fourteenth century
B. C., shows that the Hittites were gaining control of
Syria and that the security of Canaan was threatened.
It was the subsequent, steady warfare of these two
great empires for the control of these rich territories
lying between their own domains that destroyed the
Amorite-Canaanite civilizations, and substantially
weakened their own strength, thus opening the way
for the settlement of the Hebrews in Canaan. Hu-
manly speaking, this would have been impossible until
after the bitter, wasting warfare between Ramses II
and his Hittite rival, Khetasar. The other outstanding sovereignties of the thirteenth century were the
Kingdom of Mitanni between the upper Euphrates
and the Balikh, a small but influential state; Assyria,
which under Tukulti-Ninib I (about 1290–1250 B. C.),
a vigorous warrior, made a brief but noteworthy bid
for the control of Western Asia; only to be repressed
by the third, Babylonia, which was still an empire of
vast resourcefulness. These three, however, neutralized one another for a long period. No one outstanding, aggressive, imperial power appeared in Asia for
the next two centuries, a fact of much significance for
budding Hebrew nationalism.

3. **The Awakening of the Hebrews (Exodus 1 : 1–22;
2 : 23–25).**

The first chapter of Exodus is a witness to certain
interesting facts. First, the Hebrews multiplied in
numbers while they were in Egypt, becoming in reality
a considerable people. Again the reigning sovereign
of Egypt reduced them to slavery. They were treated

like captives of warfare, forced to undertake toilsome, unrequited, monumental tasks. Thus the older relations of friendship and privilege between the Egyptians and the Hebrews were replaced by hatred and hostility. Egypt thenceforth became for centuries an object of abhorrence or of satire in the mind of a Hebrew, whether peasant or statesman.

## 4. The Training of Moses for His Life Work (Exodus 2 : 1–4 : 26).

The beautiful story of Moses the deliverer interprets itself.

How the infant Moses was adopted by the daughter of the Pharaoh. Exodus 2 : 1–10.

How in early manhood he championed his own oppressed people. 2 : 11–15a.

His flight to Midian and life there in freedom and quiet. 2 : 15b–22.

His call by Jehovah to be the deliverer of his people from Egyptian servitude. 3 : 1–4 : 18.

Eliminating the passages (3 : 21–4 : 9; 4 : 19–26) which interfere with the direct progress of the narrative, the story of the preparation of Moses for his task is impressively told. Given a wonderful training as a recognized member of the royal family, he yet ranged himself when the crisis came with his own kindred, not counting the personal cost. He fled to the Midianites, a semi-nomadic people near the eastern arm of the Red Sea, whose traditions were not unlike those of his forefathers. There for many years he must have pondered over the situation of his people, laying the plans for their deliverance which gave him eventually such confident leadership.

The story of his call to public service emphasizes three commanding reasons for his willingness to ven-

ture back to Egypt on behalf of his people. At lonely
Horeb he gained a new vision of God as his friendly
Leader, adequate in power, adopting the cause of the
Hebrews, making them His own children. The new,
mysterious name of God (Exodus 3 : 14) conveyed the
idea of a gracious, active, friendly Personality.[1] With
such a conception of the Divine Being who was behind
him Moses could go ahead with confidence. Again
Moses came to feel that the time had come for the fulfilment of his plans. The old sovereign had died.
During the dozen or more years of weak government
that followed, a bold leader like Moses may well have
found his opportunity. In the third place, however,
there came to him an overwhelming sense of duty to
his people, which overruled every sort of objection he
could frame. Evidently in the desert he underwent
one of those great spiritual experiences which fashion
the leaders of any age.

5. **His Struggle with the Sovereign of Egypt Over a
Recognition of Hebrew Rights (Exodus 4 : 27–
11 : 10).**

A certain confusion is given to the mind of the close
reader of these chapters by the variations of expression. These are due, as in Genesis, to the fact that the
historical portions of these chapters represent a combination of two complete, prophetic narratives of the
exodus, with large use of the one generally regarded
as the earlier one, both supplemented by a third one
due to the priestly narrator. Each reported in its own
fashion the plagues by which the Egyptians became
convinced that the God of the Hebrews was acting
powerfully in their behalf. They agreed upon many,

[1] The divine name, usually pronounced in three syllables, Jehovah, should probably
be rendered in two, Yahweh. Since Jehovah is the more familiar form, it is retained
in this volume.

especially the culminating ones. All testified to the
call and commission of Moses, to the new conception
of God which he proclaimed, to a series of calamities
in Egypt which all attributed to the power and purpose of Jehovah, and to the sudden departure of the
Hebrews at the end of the struggle. Thus to all the
essential facts these earlier narratives give a triple testimony out of national tradition.

> How Aaron was associated with Moses in the task of deliverance.
> Exodus 4 : 27–31.
> Their first approach to the Pharaoh with a request for religious
> privilege. 5 : 1–3.
> The resultant pitiless oppression of the Hebrews. 5 : 4–6 : 1.
> [The parallel account of data already stated 6 : 2–7 : 7.]
> The series of plagues by which the Egyptians were made willing to
> let the Hebrews go. 7 : 8–10 : 20 *passim*.
> The repeated and increasingly comprehensive demands for the
> right to sacrifice as a people. 7 : 16; 8 : 1, 8, 20, 25–28; 9 : 1, 13;
> 10 : 3, 7–11, 24–26.
> The plagues which broke the Pharaoh's spirit. 10 : 21–29; 11 : 4–8;
> 12 : 29–33.

The story of the struggle between the Hebrew leaders and the powerful Pharaoh and his lords tended
naturally in Hebrew remembrance to become a narrative of marvels. The exact historical facts can never
be known, but they must have been substantially as
the Bible represents. How else could one man, however remarkable, wrest a whole people from the grip
of a power notoriously callous to all interests other than
its own! A stupendous historical miracle was cer-
tainly achieved. On the other hand, the stirring record
rightly points out the Divine share in this achievement.
It was God, not Moses, who really won the victory.
In gratitude for His work of deliverance the Hebrews
soon after declared themselves Jehovah's people.

The story of these days also indicates an extremely
skilful approach to the Pharaoh by Moses. His orig-

inal demand was for permission to lead the Hebrews
a three days' journey into the desert in order that they
might properly recognize their God. It was an entirely appropriate request on behalf of a pastoral
people to whom Egyptian soil was a foreign domain.
It did not involve a renunciation of allegiance, but did
involve a recognition of Hebrew tribal identity and of
Hebrew rights as a people. The plea was rejected
with scorn, because the Hebrews had come to be looked
upon as slaves, entitled to no consideration. Moses
continued to insist that they should be allowed to act
as a people (8 : 25–27; 10 : 8–11, 24–26) and after their
accustomed fashion. Such a plea was perfectly reasonable, and would have impressed the reasonably minded
among the Egyptians.

6. The Departure of the Hebrews from Egypt
   (Exodus 12 : 1–15 : 21).

The current of the historical narrative in Exodus is
broken somewhat by the inclusion of legislation relating to the passover celebration and to the redemption
of the first-born (12 : 1–28; 12 : 40–13 : 16), introduced
by the compiler to indicate the origin and details of
two of the fundamental customs of the Hebrews.

> The institution of the Passover as a distinctively Hebrew feast.
>   Exodus 12 : 1–16, 21–28, 43–49. [12 : 17–20.]
> The final demonstration of Jehovah's power and the hurried yield-
>   ing of the Pharaoh and his people.   12 : 29–39, [40–42; 12 : 50–
>   13 : 10].
> The law of the redemption of the first-born.   13 : 11–16.
> The departure for the desert.   13 : 17–22.
> Pharaoh's renewed attempt to enforce his will.   14 : 1–9.
> The wonderful deliverance of the Hebrews.   14 : 10–31.
> Miriam's song of thanksgiving.   15 : 20, 21, 1–11b.

Forever related in Hebrew consciousness with the
deliverance of their fathers from Egyptian bondage

were the two national observances of the Passover
and of the ransoming of the first-born. Each grew
out of earlier religious customs. Moses' demand upon
Pharaoh implied an ancient religious festival which the
Passover displaced. The recognition of God's right
to the first-fruits of nature or of the family was no new
idea. Yet these hallowed customs gained an added
sanction through the gracious and mighty providences
of God at the time of the deliverance.

The estimate of the number of the people who es-
caped from Egypt, given in Exodus 12 : 37 (reiterated
in Numbers 1 : 46; 26 : 51), implies about two millions
in all. This number seems much too large in view of
the actual conditions of the desert, and because of
casual hints in the later Biblical narrative (Exodus
23 : 30; Numbers 13 : 31; Judges 5 : 8). The large estimates came from the priestly writer, whose sense of
God's power was so profound that difficulties were
ignored.

The wonder of the deliverance was ever foremost in
the Hebrew mind. It was Jehovah's thoughtful care,
they realized, that made it possible. The probabilities
were all against success. The Hebrews might have
taken the direct "way of the land of the Philistines,"
the ancient route to Canaan, but fortunately they did
not try this route. It would have invited fresh perils.
The "way of the wilderness" ran directly eastward to
the desert which they desired to reach. This edge of
Egypt was protected by a line of garrisoned fortresses
from Lake Timsah to the Mediterranean. The narrative seems to imply that the Hebrews were obliged to
try to skirt this barrier, and were caught between the
pursuing Egyptian army and the shallow arm of the
Red Sea. Here the way across was suddenly made
possible, whereas the pursuing chariots were over-

whelmed. The uprising of the walls of water on either side, making a lane of dry land through a sea of some depth (14 : 29) is a poetical conception, not in accord with the more prosaic but no less providential blowing back of the shallow waters of the arm of the sea by a heavy wind from the east (14 : 21).

However the Hebrews got across the bar between Egypt and the free desert, that achievement was the birthday of the Hebrew people. All sense of obligation to Egypt had been cancelled. The influence and authority of Moses had been established. Above all, the people had gained an unfading conviction that Jehovah had delivered them, and that they ought to accept His leadership and protection and become His people.

7. The Leadership of Moses at Sinai (Exodus 15 : 22–24 : 18; 32–35, passim).

The story of the period which intervenes between the departure from Egypt and the arrival in Canaan is hard to unravel from the perplexingly varied contents of Exodus, Leviticus, Numbers, and Deuteronomy. The order in which things happened is often far from clear. On the other hand, certain outstanding facts are unquestionable. The stay at Sinai was the time when the Hebrew people became inspirited by Moses for their national task. What he accomplished is often overestimated in its details, but never in its significance. The Hebrew people emerged at this time from the near-heathenism into which they had lapsed and learned to worship one good, gracious, holy God.

The march to Sinai. Exodus 15 : 22–16 : 1; 17 : 1; 19 : 1–2.
The school of thankful obedience. 16 : 2–17 : 7.
The solemn blood compact with Jehovah at Sinai. 19 : 3–25.

The giving of the sacred ceremonial code, the "Ten Words."
34 : 10–28.

The great ethical code.  20 : 1–17 (Deuteronomy 5 : 6–21).

The joyful construction of the sacred Tent of Meeting as a dwelling-
place for Jehovah, and its usefulness.  25 : 1, 8; 35 : 21; 36 : 2,
3a, 8a; 33 : 7–11.

Jehovah's gracious and wonderful manifestation of His Presence to
Moses.  33 : 17, 12–16, 19, 18, 20–23; 34 : 5–9.

At Sinai Moses was faced by a stupendous task.
He had to fuse into a working unity a group of clans
and families unaccustomed to cooperation.  He accomplished this by subjecting them to a powerful religious impulse, loyalty to Jehovah their Deliverer,
henceforth to be their Leader.  The basis of the covenant was simple enough, yet it was ethical.  He would
guide and protect them; they would worship Him.
The whole value of it, religiously speaking, lay in the
character of Jehovah.  At Sinai few besides Moses
were able to appreciate His true nature; the people had
to realize it gradually, even through centuries.

Moses drove home at Sinai a few fundamental facts
about Jehovah.  He was powerful, gracious, able to
care for them, but moral in His demands.  Injustice
and wrongdoing He would punish; integrity, truthful-
ness, and purity he expected in His followers.  He and
they were to stand together exclusively.  All this was
ethical more than spiritual; it was not yet the enlightened monotheism of centuries later, but it made a
strong start toward it.

The remainder of Exodus is given to details of legislation into which we need not enter.  It is generally
agreed to-day that the legislation found in Exodus,
Leviticus, Numbers, and Deuteronomy is a complex
of many legislative codes of different ages, representing the gradual development of Mosaic institutions
during a period of over seven hundred years.  The earli-

est and simplest may be Exodus 34 : 14–26, which is a
primitive but distinctly religious code. Whether the
code of 20 : 2–17 is equally early is one of the hotly
argued questions of Biblical scholarship. As now
placed in the record this little code seems to have been
an insertion, since 20 : 1 contradicts 20 : 19, and breaks
the connection between 19 : 17 and 20 : 18. Yet by
its definitely ethical character it supplements the other
short code. Its lofty standards cause some students to
date it later than David, but this reason does not seem
conclusive. That the fundamental principles on which
Moses desired their life as a people to be based should
be expressed in short, simple codes like these is wholly
in accordance with probabilities. The longer code of
Exodus 20 : 23–23 : 19 is so clearly a code for community
life that it seems to represent the life in Canaan.

At Sinai Moses gained the acceptance of the covenant
with Jehovah by the people, made provision for His
regular worship at a simple sanctuary, and established
regulations which insured sanitation, public order,
health, and cooperative action. His people were still
mainly slaves in spirit. They needed simple institutions which they could understandingly obey. He was
fortunate in his lieutenants. There must have been,
besides Joshua, a good many dependable ones (24 : 14),
whose names are unknown, through whom Moses was
able to begin the task of training his people into a God-
fearing race in whose minds religion of a high and noble
sort should become established.

**8. The Wilderness Years (Exodus, Numbers, and
Deuteronomy, passim).**

To trace the history of these years with accuracy is
quite out of the question. The Hebrews made Kadesh
their headquarters, but must have roamed much of the

time about the southern desert in their old fashion.
Yet the great blessing they craved was a homeland,
where they could live in peace. Toward Canaan they
were moving in heart and in fact. Only the outstanding events need be traced below.

> The journey to Kadesh. Deuteronomy 1 : 6–19.
> The abortive attempt to invade Canaan from the south. Numbers
>     13, 14; Deuteronomy 1 : 20–46.
> The judicial organization of the people. Deuteronomy 1 : 9–17;
>     Exodus 18.
> The refusal of Edom to give a right of way. Numbers 20 : 14–21.
> The conquest of the Amorites and discomfiture of Amalek.
>     Exodus 17 : 8–15; Numbers 21 : 21–32; Deuteronomy 2 : 24–36.
> How Balaam, the seer, hired by Moab to put a curse upon the He-
>     brews, was forced to follow God's will. Numbers 22 : 2–35.
> His predictions of Israel's greatness. Numbers 22 : 36–24 : 25.
> The East-Jordan tribes settled yet loyal. Numbers 32.
> The last days of Moses. Numbers 27 : 12–23; Deuteronomy 31,
>     32, 34.

During the long delay while Kadesh was their headquarters, a process of organization was going on, reported in Exodus 18 as taking place even before the
events at Sinai, but by Deuteronomy 1 as occurring
later. The exact date is less important than the fact,
which illustrated the boundless energy and capacity
of Moses. He may have been fortunate in his advisers,
but he was, after all, responsible for a scheme of government which substituted orderliness for confusion, de-
centralized the administration of common justice, and
gave a substantial, civil unity to a rather clannish people.

Out of the perplexing and often conflicting historical details embodied in these records, which are primarily legal, emerge several indisputable data, such as
the removal to Kadesh, the premature and unsuccessful attempt to penetrate Canaan from the south, the
refusal of Edom to give a right of way to the East-
Jordan country, the circuit around Edom, various suc-

cessful encounters with determined foes, the anxiety
of Moab over the appearance of the militant new-
comers, and the ultimate arrival at a point whence the
entrance into Canaan was feasible. It is the danger
of the Biblical reader that he overestimates the unity
of the Hebrew tribes in these transactions. To what
extent these achievements were accomplished by the
group of tribes working together or by separate groups
acting on their own initiative is quite uncertain. The
Hebrew writers were themselves viewing these years
through a veil of dim tradition. The one supremely
important fact is that during the long sojourn at
Kadesh these tribesmen with separate family affiliations and peculiar customs gained a sense of religious
unity and a definite though simple religious stamp
which was able to survive the tremendous testing of
the fierce struggles of the next one hundred years.

9. **The Significant Place of Moses in Hebrew History.**

. The book of Deuteronomy concludes the record of
the life of Moses with the judgment that he was unique
among men of prophetic power (Deuteronomy 34:10),
a well-deserved tribute to the essential element in his
greatness in history. He had a real vision of God and
passed along a genuine message from Him to those of
his generation. But Moses was more than an interpreter. He had the especial and rare genius of a
founder. He initiated the greatest course of religious
growth the world has ever known. This was due to
his prophetic qualities. What he put into motion was
simple enough. It had to be so in order to fit the vital
needs of the simple-minded people he led. But he
looked ahead, not only organizing soundly, but establishing ideals that persisted and blossomed vigorously.

His greatest fitness for his task was not his commanding personality or his patient devotedness to a trying, impulsive, intractable people. It did not grow out of his superior cultural advantage or through his unusual experience. It rested clearly on the illuminating visions of God (Exodus 3, 33, 34) which gave him such power of religious leadership that the people could only hold that Moses was privileged to see Him "face to face." He was able to kindle a faith in this righteous and good, yet powerful Jehovah and a willingness to enlist under Him which were both vital and persistent.

The real history of the Hebrew people begins with Moses, their accepted leader, the wise organizer of their institutional life, the watchful guardian of their interests, and the interpreter of their future. On the basis which he laid was reared the essential structure of their whole national life. Later generations made no real mistake in attributing to him the whole body of results developed during the next seven centuries.

# III

## THE GRADUAL NATIONALIZATION OF
## THE HEBREW PEOPLE

### JOSHUA TO I KINGS 11 (ABOUT 1150–937 B. C.)

The crossing of the Jordan, whether accomplished in a day or during a generation, marked a decisive turning point in the life of the Hebrews as a people. In place of being semi-nomadic they mainly settled down to village life; they exchanged the keeping of flocks for agricultural pursuits; their social and religious habits were altered in many important respects; eventually they achieved true nationality. That these changes were, on the whole, for the better can hardly be questioned. The Hebrews took a step upward in civilization. It was also a step ahead in religion. The Canaanites were a more highly organized people. The adoption of their customs introduced some very serious evils into Hebrew life; yet on the whole the new viewpoints were such as to give the Hebrews a better chance to develop a wisely organized life. These two centuries were clearly the age of establishment in a suitable home and of organization for future nationality. At their close the Hebrew people were just beginning their real national life.

### 1. The Canaan of the Twelfth Century B. C.

The records of Egypt and Babylonia attest the existence of a relatively high civilization in Canaan during several centuries just preceding the Hebrew invasion.

This was the fruitage of more than a thousand years of settled occupancy of Canaan, always sensitive to the cultural influences of western Asia. The Canaanites dwelt in houses in walled "cities." In government, manner of life, commerce, and religion they were in their own way proficient. But the recurrence of devastating warfare between Egypt and the Hittites up and down their entire country gradually weakened them so greatly that the aggressive Hebrews became formidable opponents, able to meet the better organized inhabitants of Canaan on terms which were fairly even.

Canaan was the early name of the land which we call Palestine. It was approximately the size of Vermont. Much of this limited area was unproductive or barren. It had a central mountainous backbone paralleling the sea, sloping off gradually into the southern desert and putting forth many little ridges which disappeared into the coastal plain. The mountain range opened south of the Sea of Galilee to make a clear passageway from the Syrian plains to the coast. From the "hill country" the Hebrews could observe the traffic and hear the news of the world of their day. At the same time the varied configuration of the land afforded both a wide variety of climate and condition and provided many secluded spots where a group of people could live unmolested by ordinary wayfarers. Such a situation explains the presence of fragments of different peoples in Canaan at the time of the Hebrew invasion. (Exodus 23 : 23.)

Fortunately for the Hebrews, Canaan was free from overwhelming attack for nearly two centuries after they occupied it. About 1120 B. C. a great Assyrian sovereign, Tiglath-pileser I, made the name of Assyria widely feared by reason of his aggressive prowess. He pushed his victories westward to the Mediterranean near Aleppo, but did not continue southward toward Egypt. His reign, however, was luckily followed by those of far weaker sovereigns until the ninth century. During this long interval the other great Asiatic powers were either, like the Arameans, finding themselves, or, like Egypt, unaggressive.

## 2. The Hebrew Conquest of Canaan (Joshua, Judges).

The story of the gradual settlement of Canaan by the Hebrews is reflected rather than related by the records found in the Books of Joshua and Judges. The exact details are far from clear. Historians of later days foreshortened the sequence of events and often idealized them. It is fairly certain that the conquest of Canaan was neither so speedy an event, nor so unified or complete as the reader of Joshua 1–12 would infer. The process was rather, as Exodus 23 : 30 and Deuteronomy 7 : 22 put it, "by little and little." The entrance may have been by infiltration as well as by conquest, from more points of approach than Jericho, and during some portion of a half century. Eventually, however, the Hebrews were settled on both sides of the Jordan and had as serious opponents only small groups of Canaanites and the Philistines.

The preparations of Joshua, the new Hebrew leader, for the capture of Jericho. Joshua 1, 2.
The crossing of the Jordan by his forces. 3 : 1–5 : 1.
Their capture of Jericho. 5 : 13–6 : 27.
The sweeping punishment of Achan and his family for his theft. 7.
The capture of Ai by Joshua. 8.
How the Gibeonites saved themselves by a stratagem. 9.
The defeat of the five allied kings at Bethhoron. 10 : 1–27.
The defeat of Jabin and his coalition. 11 : 1–15.
Traditions which may reflect early incursions into Canaan. Genesis 34, 38.
Another story of the advance of Judah and Simeon. Judges 1 : 1–21.

The capture of Bethel by the Joseph tribes.  1 : 22–26.
The many reverses and partial failures of the Hebrew aggressors.
  1 : 27–36.
The (Deuteronomic editor's) summary of the conquest.  Joshua
  10 : 28–43; 11 : 10–23.
The (Deuteronomic editor's) interpretation of the conquest.
  Judges 2 : 6–3 : 6.
The (very late) account of the division and organization of the
  land and of Joshua's farewell.  Joshua 13–24.

The plain language of Judges 1 : 19, 21, 27–36 is
enough to show that the summary of the Deuteronomic compiler in Joshua 11 : 10-23 was idealized.  The
actual conquest was not as complete as therein indicated.  Joshua and others broke down opposition and
gained a secure foothold, but were far from becoming
at once the masters of Canaan.  Their keen desire for
settled homes and the unity of attack developed under
good leadership and a belief in Jehovah's protection
gave them a real advantage.  Yet the Canaanites held
onto a number of strategic centres and much of the
fertile territory for a long time.  The Hebrews ultimately formed four rather distinct groups, that on the
east of the Jordan, that in the extreme south, the central tribes, and the northern tribes.  These divisions
may have come about through independent advances
into Canaan from different directions or through the
curious fact that in Joshua's day and later a line of
Canaanitish fortified towns separated Judah from the
central hill country, and another line cut off the central region of western Canaan from that of the north,
while of course the Jordan River served as a natural
line of demarcation.

Gradually, almost imperceptibly, by peaceful infiltration and through intermarriage and incorporation,
the Hebrews absorbed the Canaanites completely, assuming their ways of living, adopting much of their
civilization and accepting many of their religious habits

and shrines. The later Deuteronomic editors of the book of Judges (Judges 2 : 6–3 : 6) regarded this wholesale incorporation of the Canaanites and adoption of their ways as indicating a religious collapse. The verdict of Biblical history as a whole is otherwise. For a people groping its way out of social clannishness and the simple though often austere religious ideas which it encourages, the new life of Canaan marked a real advance, not alone socially and culturally, but also religiously. Community and household religion represent a more wholesome type than religion on the march. The real danger to the Hebrews lay in their possible failure to interpret and direct the new, broadened life by Mosaic principles.

In this process they had the invaluable aid of good leaders. Joshua in Hebrew tradition was a soldier with a soldier's good and bad traits. Courage, promptness, earnestness, simplicity, and faith were his natural virtues. He was a faithful guardian of the interests transmitted to him by Moses and a loyal supporter of Mosaic ideals. He not only won for his people a homeland, but also kept alive their loyalty to Jehovah.

3. **The Sporadic Leadership in the Days of the " Judges " (Judges 3 : 7–12 : 15; Ruth).**

During the century or more of the gradual transfer of Canaan to Hebrew possession, the loosely united confederacy, while fortunately safe from the attacks of powerful empires, was still in constant danger. Groups of tribes were frequently obliged to meet enemies of their own strength. The Hebrews became hardy, seasoned fighters (Judges 3 : 1–4) who set a high value on physical prowess. They ascribed their good fortune to the protection of Jehovah, and grew in con-

36     OLD TESTAMENT HISTORY

fidence and loyalty.  When a crisis came, a leader
sprang up to meet it.

Othniel the Kenizzite deliverer.  Judges 3:7–11.
The victory of Ehud, the left-handed Benjamite, over the Moab-
    ites.  3:12–30; and the exploit of Shamgar.  3:31.
The migration of the Danites and founding of the famous shrine
    at Dan.  17, 18.
The moral outrage at Gibeah and punishment of Benjamin by the
    tribesmen.  19–21.
The victory of Deborah and Barak over the Canaanites.  4:1–22.
Deborah's stirring and patriotic battle ode.  5.
Gideon's great victory over the Midianitish marauders.  6–8.
The abortive reign of Abimelech in Shechem.  9.
Jepthah's campaign against the Ammonites: his fatal vow and its
    tragic outcome.  10:6–12:7.
Minor deliverers.  10:1–5; 12:8–15.
The idyllic story of the adoption of Ruth, the Moabitess, into the
    tribe of Judah.  Ruth 1–4.

This was a stirring century.  The Hebrew clansmen
were crude, rough, ambitious, often unscrupulous.
They seemed in truth to be doing, each one, what was
"right in his own eyes."  Three advantages kept them
growing in the upward direction.  First were their
leaders.  Over against a Shamgar or an Ehud we may
place a heroic, large-minded, great-hearted Deborah
or a persistently faithful Naomi, a respected and influential Boaz, or a bold, ingenious, intrepid Gideon,
modest in victory, loyal to Jehovah, representing the
Hebrew at his best.  Again their Mosaic traditions
were kept alive by the presence of the ark with its
symbols of worship and by the codes of accepted law
which carried divine sanction.  In the third place, their
underlying loyalty to Jehovah as their accepted God
persisted.  This loyalty was often nominal, yet an appeal to it produced results.  A really astonishing series
of violations of the moral law is related in connection
with the seizure by the Danites of Micah's prized sanctuary (Judges 17, 18), yet unquestionably the tribe

keenly desired a regular means of giving Jehovah his proper worship. Even so high-handed a procedure indicates that they valued Jehovah's favor. Their ideas of Him were still very crude. Jepthah (Judges 11 : 23, 24) ranked Chemosh with Jehovah. The great prophetic idealism was still centuries in the future.

4. **The Philistine Menace and Its Awakening Influence on the Hebrews (Judges 13–16; I Samuel 1 : 1–7 : 17).**
What forced the Hebrew tribes to exchange their valued independence for a closer organization was an increasingly powerful enemy close at hand. The Philistines had gained a foothold in the fertile coast plain at about the time when the Hebrews began to enter Canaan, or slightly before. They were a sturdy, aggressive, well-organized, federated group of related peoples, farther advanced in culture than the Hebrews, and their most dangerous foe. Fortunately they were not strong enough to take the aggressive until the Hebrews had largely assimilated the remaining Canaanites, had developed some sense of unity as a people, were ready to follow able leaders, and believed that Jehovah at Shiloh, the sanctuary where the ark remained, was their protecting presence. The time came, however, after about a century of occupation, when the Philistines made a successful offensive.

The incidental warfare with the Philistines represented by the exploits of Samson. Judges 13–16.
The high quality of the parentage and early training of Samuel. I Samuel 1 : 1–2 : 11.
How Samuel in his youth came to be recognized as a man of God. 2 : 12–4 : 1a.
The successful campaign of the Philistines against the Hebrews of the central highlands. 4 : 1b–7 : 3.
A late tradition that Samuel threw off this yoke. 7 : 3–17.

The dates to be assigned to these events are so uncertain that no student can declare with entire confidence their actual course. Probably the Philistines followed up their victory by establishing military posts which enabled them to control the conquered territory and to collect tribute (I Samuel 10:5; 13:3, 23; 14:1, 11). They also disarmed the Hebrews (13:19–22). When Saul was found by Samuel the Hebrews were still groaning under the Philistine yoke, and the fortresses were still in use. How to reconcile these facts with the story of Samuel's victory (7:5–14) is not clear.

Over against this story of disaster may be placed its moral value. Samson was no more than a playful giant, rejoicing that his strength and wit enabled him to annoy or circumvent these enemies of his people. Eli, the aged priest, weak of will yet with clear prescience of the trend of events, regretted bitterly the wasted energies of his people. He saw that they needed, for their proper unification and deliverance, the leadership of a personality like Samuel, born out of the best Israelitish stock, from God-fearing parents. Hannah, Naomi, and Ruth are among the answers to the charge of the unrelieved moral and spiritual crudeness of the age. Samuel represented the highest product of Hebrew conditions. He embodied for his countrymen their best and therefore won their confidence. Through him they made a fresh and vigorous start toward real political unity. He also must be credited with the organization of the prophets into an order which played a noteworthy part in Israel's future. His rule was not merely a political or social progress; it was a moral and spiritual step in advance. It represented the union of social, political, and religious aims.

5. Saul's Deliverance of the Hebrews from the Philistine Yoke and His Early Reign (I Samuel
8–14).

Samuel's greatest service to the Hebrew people was
not his guidance of their affairs before Saul's reign, but
his choice of Saul as the first king, and his insistence
upon kingly standards. He is represented in I Samuel
8 : 11–18 as having his doubts about the happy outcome of the establishment of a kingdom, but he knew,
as all now thought, that it represented the next step
to take. He found with God's help the one who
seemed to be the right man. Saul finely justified that
judgment in his early reign.

The eagerness of the Hebrews for a king and Samuel's warning.
I Samuel 8.
How Samuel found Saul and consecrated him to the kingly office.
9 : 1–10 : 16.
How Saul's fitness for the leadership of the people became mani-
fest, so that he was crowned king at Gilgal. 10 : 17–11 : 15.
A late interpretation of Samuel's attitude. 12.
Saul's successful campaign against the Philistines. 13 : 1–14 : 46.
His aggressive early reign. 14 : 47–52.

Saul was outwardly and inwardly an excellent choice
as the ruler of such a people. He was more like a
Scottish chieftain in his methods and ideas than a
reigning sovereign. His palace was his ancestral home,
his hall of justice the shade of an oak-tree, his sceptre
a spear, his courtiers his family retainers (I Samuel
22 : 6). His summons to war was by a primitive
method (11 : 7). He ruled by right of prowess and
personality (9 : 2). He had dreamed of freeing his
countrymen (9 : 19c). With his splendid son, Jonathan, he led his subjects to victory, not merely clearing
the Philistines from Hebrew territory, but dealing decisively with other aggressive peoples (14 : 47, 48). In

all this he met their expectations and drew out their
enthusiasm and loyalty. But he was as superstitious
as Jepthah (14 : 43, 44), not really fitting into the great
historic succession of leaders.

## 6. David's Career at Court and in Camp (I Samuel 15-31).

Saul's success turned his head. He became so wil-
ful and self-assertive that the old relations of confidence
and friendship between him and Samuel were broken.
Just when this occurred no one can say. The narrative prefers to emphasize the next great forward step
of nationalization, the discovery of David, the real
creator of Hebrew statehood, beside whom Saul was
an amateur. It also emphasizes the varied experiences
through which the attractive, brave, and skilful youth,
David, became the resourceful, broad-minded, popular,
statesmanlike sovereign. His fitness was not wholly
a matter of good qualities; it was in considerable measure due to seized opportunity.

How Saul and Samuel were estranged. I Samuel 15.
How Samuel was led to consecrate David for national leadership.
   16 : 1-13.
How David was summoned to Saul's court and prospered there.
   16 : 14-18 : 5. (Earliest narrative. 16 : 14-23; 17 : 1-11, 32-40,
   42-54.)
The gradual growth of a spirit of jealousy in Saul's mind. 18 : 6-
   19 : 24.
David's forced retirement from the court to the wilderness. 20-23.
His growing recognition by the nation as a leader to be trusted.
   24, 25.
Saul's relentless pursuit of David, who flees to Gath of Philistia
   but remains true to Hebrew interests. 26, 27.
The new Philistine invasion and the death of Saul on Mt. Gilboa.
   28-31.

The David of these days had far to go as an ideal
leader, but was ripening. He believed in vigorous

methods and was not overscrupulous in the means he used (18 : 27; 21 : 5; 25 : 22; 27 : 11). He outwitted those who matched themselves with him. The primitiveness of his religious ideas is shown by the fact that he seemed to believe that when he was driven away from Hebrew soil he had left Jehovah behind (26 : 19). But he was gradually surrounded by a fine group of men (22 : 1, 2, 5, 20), courtiers, prophets, and priests. Moreover he had the priceless treasure of the unrestricted devotion of a man like Jonathan, whose noble character quickened his own (20 : 12–17, 23, 41, 42; 23 : 16–18). Best of all he was enabled to render such services to his countrymen that Abigail could hail him as the sure successor of Saul (25 : 28–31) and a real leader of the people. His future was sure.

**7.  The Creative Nationalizing Work of David as King of all Israel (II Samuel 1–24).**

The death of Saul and his sons gave David a sudden prominence. Saul's hold upon his subjects, however, was such that Ishbaal, a son of his, with the help of a fine soldier, Abner, retained the throne of Israel for some years. David was chosen king in Judah, but both he and Ishbaal were probably vassals of the Philistines. The death of Ishbaal opened the way for David to become king of all Israel. At once he began to show his fitness to wield this authority. Having subdued the Philistines speedily and decisively, he captured the fortress of Jebus and founded a capital, Jerusalem. This small city he rapidly made into a real capital, the centre of all Israelitish life, political, social, and religious. He organized the people into a nation with such success that the Hebrews speedily dominated their small part of the world. He thus gave them the real characteristics of nationalism, a sense of independence and an outlook.

David's sincere grief over the death of Saul and Jonathan.  II
  Samuel 1 : 1–27.
His quick acceptance as king of Judah.  2 : 1–4.
The seven years' interval before the death of Ishbaal.  2 : 5–4 : 12.
The coronation of David as king over all Israel.  5 : 1–5.
His capture of Jerusalem which was made a true capital.  5 : 6–16;
  6 : 1–23; 8 : 15–18.
The speedy and skilful crushing of the Philistines.  5 : 17–25;
  21 : 15–22; 23 : 9–17.
His conquests of surrounding peoples.  8 : 1–14; 10 : 1–19.
His kindness to the son of Jonathan.  9 : 1–13; 16 : 1–4; 19 : 24–30;
  21 : 7.
David's deplorable sin and its long train of bitter personal conse-
  quences.  11–20.
Incidents showing his primitiveness of thinking.  21, 24.

David's portrait in these chapters is a many-sided
one.  He stands out as a skilful leader in warfare and
a genius in statecraft.  He set up a real kingdom without delay, one well adapted to the needs of his people.
This kingdom he organized, simply but adequately.
He was generous to some foes, terrible to others.  He
won the loyalty of all, even of old foes (15 : 19–22).
The greater portion of the matchless historical narrative
which tells the story of his reign is given to the account
of his moral downfall and its many consequences.
Despite his sincere repentance, it wrecked his life.

What he was religiously is more of a question.
These narratives, carefully read, do not give him a
high religious rating.  He was thoroughly loyal to Jehovah; he longed to render Him some signal service,
such as the erection of a suitable temple; but he still
was swayed by superstition as primitive as that which
influenced Jepthah (21 : 1–14).  Although he surely
possessed the soul of a poet (1 : 17–26), and while he
thought it worth his while to add a "chronicler" to the
officials of his court (8 : 16), yet there are many difficulties in the way of regarding his reign as a brilliant
literary era.  It made a strong start.

## 8. The Dangerously Ambitious Reign of Solomon, His Son (I Kings 1–11).

David's reign was long and, notwithstanding the rebellions recorded, his grip upon the throne was secure. He transferred the crown to Solomon, the son of Bathsheba. His choice seemed a good one. Few sovereigns showed greater promise than Solomon. He had a real genius for reigning. His fame as a sovereign rests chiefly upon the building of the beautiful temple for the unseen Jehovah, which immediately exercised a great and growing influence on the religious life of the people. It should rest also upon Solomon's schemes for promoting and protecting commerce, upon his beautification of the capital, upon his political affiliations and his encouragement of culture. His weakness lay in the inordinate ambition which eventually possessed him. This made him crave a place in the world like that of the great sovereigns of Egypt and elsewhere. His inability to resist this fascinating passion caused him to wreck the fortunes of his people. He taxed them into revolt.

The sudden selection of Solomon as David's successor and his coronation. I Kings 1 : 1–53.
Solomon's evident fitness to rule. 2 : 1–3 : 28.
The organization of his kingdom and court. 4.
His building of the splendid temple for Jehovah. 5–7.
The solemn dedication of the temple to the worship of the Invisible. 8 : 1–9 : 9.
Solomon's many enterprises. 9 : 10–28.
How his whole world praised him and contributed to his glory. 10 : 1–29.
The evil side of his many alliances. 11 : 1–13.
His minor adversaries. 11 : 14–25.
How the prophet Ahijah predicted a revolt under Jeroboam. 11 : 26–40.
The close of Solomon's long and peaceful reign. 11 : 41–43.

Solomon, like David, was idealized by posterity. In his case also there was much justification. Solomon was a remarkable ruler of real genius.  He should have been the sovereign of an empire with vast resources. His ideas outreached his judgment.  They were not unsound but beyond the resources of his people.  His subjects became more and more discontented.  Their taxes and contributions seemed unbearable.  Thus he seemed to have wrecked by his obstinacy and selfish imperialism that national unity for which his father, David, had labored so earnestly.

## 9.  The Newly Created Hebrew Nation.

But no one can wholly wreck progress once truly made.  The Hebrews had been drawn into a real working unit by David.  They had achieved triumphs over other peoples through that unity.  They had rejoiced with him over the power of Jehovah on their behalf. They had a visible centre of national life at Jerusalem, not only a capital and a court but a reminder of their religious loyalty.  They had gained self-confidence as a people, and were ready to develop in future days a real national programme.  Except for the popular discontent over Solomon's ambitious schemes, the Hebrew outlook was bright at the close of his reign.

With great probability the reigns of David and Solomon may be regarded as the era of the beginnings of Hebrew literature.  Before their day there were lacking the necessary factors.  But with the growth of the prophetic order and of the priesthood and with the development of a national feeling, cultural influences were encouraged.  Hero stories which had passed orally began to find written form.  Collections of rude poems like the "Book of the Words of Jehovah" or "Jashar" were made.  The recorder of the events of the reign of each monarch became an important court official.

Socially this century witnessed a fine development. The Hebrews were a free people, selecting their rulers. They welcomed a king as a wise means of self-protection, but were unwilling to obey a despot. On the whole, David embodied the nation's ideal.

Religiously it was a century of advance. The building of the Temple gave a visible centre to the worship of the invisible Jehovah. It helped to spiritualize and dignify the religious life of every Hebrew. Thus by 937 B. C. the Hebrew nation was well on its way.

# IV

## THE CENTURY OF REDEDICATION TO MOSAIC IDEALS

I Kings 12 : 1–II Kings 10 : 28 (937–840 B. C.)

With the achievement of nationalism the real history of the Hebrews as a people began. The forces making for culture and progress had freer course. This important attainment unexpectedly became a second great turning-point in the history of the people. A large share of Solomon's subjects revolted from his son, Rehoboam, and set up an independent dynasty of their own, which came to be known as the Northern kingdom, or, to adopt their own rather presuming title, as Israel. Only Judah, the Southern kingdom, remained loyal to the Davidic dynasty.

The story of the next three and a half centuries is told in Kings, an editorial survey of the whole period, based on annalistic notes about the kings and their reigns, enlivened by vivid stories like those about Elijah and Elisha and other prophets. Some other data are contributed from Chronicles, which are an elaboration and reinterpretation from an ideal religious view-point of the material in Kings. The modern historian is able to check these histories by the appropriate prophetic books, and by the statements of the Assyro-Babylonian records.

The first of these centuries included the inevitable

half century of adjustment—a period of warfare, assertiveness, experiment. The two kingdoms then got together reasonably well, and each met the great religious crisis imposed by the ambitious Phœnician queen and her daughter. The reaction of each Hebrew people to this crisis was the outstanding fact of the century.

1. **The Disruption of the Kingdom of Solomon (I Kings 12 : 1-24).   937 B. C.**

It seems at first sight incredible that the kingdom established under David and Solomon should be divided so easily. Events showed that the process of uniting the separative forces and conditions had been incomplete. Local jealousies and rivalries had merely been minimized in the enthusiasm of united conquest and of national zeal. During the peaceful reign of Solomon they had an opportunity, and quite possibly an excuse, for reassertion, since Solomon was suspected of favoring Judah at the expense of the rest of his kingdom. The compelling reasons, however, for the break were Solomon's ambitions, and the consequent burdens which his subjects felt acutely. They did not dare to disobey Solomon, but demanded relief from his successor, who betrayed an equally despotic temper. Reacting alike against this denial of public rights and their particular grievance, his would-be subjects revolted.

> The national assembly at Shechem to confirm Rehoboam as king and its plea for relief.  I Kings 12 : 1-5.
> Rehoboam's fatuous reply to the assembly's demand.  12 : 6-15.
> The entire renunciation of allegiance by the "ten tribes."  12 : 16-20.
> Shemaiah's counsel to Rehoboam to forego civil warfare.  12 : 21-24.

The disruption had important consequences. It substituted in place of a power which promised to have

a wide-ranging influence two small kingdoms which
merely opposed and neutralized each other. It seemed
to break up the sense of unity which had been attained.
It even opened the way to religious degeneracy. On
the other hand, it really marked a step forward. It
saved the democratic spirit, so characteristic and vital,
which enabled prophetic institutions to flourish. It
resulted in two closely related yet distinguishable kingdoms, Judah, the smaller one, conservative in habit by
reason of its royal house, its temple, and its traditions;
the other, Israel, with the majority of the people and of
the resources, progressive in spirit, sometimes recklessly
so. Their natural rivalry along with their kinship
made for a real and rapid national progress.

2. **Jeroboam's Shrewd but Short-sighted Schemes for
Establishing the New Kingdom (I Kings 12 : 25–
14 : 20).**

The new sovereign, Jeroboam, placed on the throne of
Israel by the revolting tribes, was as shrewd as David
had been in establishing what he had gained. He lost
no time in so organizing his new kingdom that its interests quickly became distinct from those of Judah.
He recognized two national sanctuaries, at the extreme
south and north, and set up in each a golden bull as
representing Jehovah. This was a distinct concession
to the Canaanitish idolatry, which was much to the
liking of many of his subjects. It was the "sin" for
which he was often denounced by the prophets and
writers of his day and later. The stories told about
him emphasize their attitude. Jeroboam likewise altered the date of the most popular festival and set up
his own priesthood.

How Jeroboam made the Northern kingdom religiously independent. I Kings 12 : 25–33.

THE CENTURY OF REDEDICATION    49

How his attitude was variously rebuked.   13 : 1–14 : 18.
His long reign.   14 : 19, 20.

Jeroboam probably regarded his religious policy as
being both timely and essential. He looked at the
matter as a politician might. It was shrewd and effi-
cacious. His people quickly forgot Jerusalem or the
temple. But Jeroboam deliberately sacrificed a higher
good for the sake of gaining an immediate advantage.
The temple with its holy of holies represented the unseen Jehovah, while these images, erected by Jeroboam,
encouraged a lapse from Mosaic idealism. For the
sake of political advantage Jeroboam sacrificed spiri-
tuality. This was truly a capital sin, because of its
consequences. He became known as the arch-inciter
of his nation to that habit of mind that proved its ruin.

3.  The First Half Century of Desultory Conflict Between the Two Kingdoms (I Kings 14 : 21–
16 : 28; II Chronicles 11–16).   937–887.

| JUDAH | ISRAEL |
|---|---|
| Rehoboam, 937–920[1] | Jeroboam I, 937–915 |
| Abijam, 920–917 | Nadab, 915–913 |
| Asa, 917–876 | Baasha, 913–889 |
| | Elah, 889–887 |
| | Zimri, 887 |
| | Omri, 887–875 |

The first half century of the existence of the two
little kingdoms side by side was principally a time of
constant clashes between them. They found it difficult to settle down. Jeroboam shifted his capital to
Penuel across the Jordan (12 : 25), possibly because
of Rehoboam's vigorous attacks (14 : 30) upon Shechem.

[1] Regnal dates are arrived at under various computations. They are approximately accurate. No student need be disturbed to find another estimate varying
from these by several years.

Jeroboam's son, Nadab, after a very short reign, was murdered by Baasha, one of his generals, who founded a new dynasty. Baasha was a vigorous warrior whose principal exploit was blockading Judah in the days of Asa by fortifying Ramah and stopping all trade. Asa countered by bribing Benhadad of Damascus, Baasha's nearest neighbor and rival, to become his own ally, urging him to attack Baasha's possessions (15 : 18–21) along the northern border. Baasha had to withdraw to Tirzah, which had become the capital of the Northern kingdom. Baasha's son and successor, Elah, after a brief reign was murdered by Zimri, one of his officers, who in turn after a week's reign was forced to self-destruction by Omri, the general, who had been elected king by the army. Thus in fifty years three dynasties, with a total of five kings, had reigned over Israel, a troubled, unfruitful, bloody period of the strong hand, presaging ill success for the new state.

Meanwhile in Judah the situation was at first deplorable, then improved. Rehoboam lived up to specifications. He permitted the Canaanitish Baalism, to which many of his subjects in Jerusalem were devoted in their hearts, to have full sway. He felt the effects of a plundering raid by Shishak of Egypt. His son, Abijam, ruled without special incident. Asa, his successor, was an able king and a real reformer. He rigorously rooted out the Canaanitish emblems (15 : 13) and purified the temple from its encouragements to vice. When Baasha tried to blockade his trade Asa bribed Benhadad of Damascus to interfere. He thus purchased temporary freedom with a permanent license to plunder. It was a blunder of great magnitude.

How Rehoboam permitted Baalism and was plundered by Shishak of Egypt and warred continually with Jeroboam. I Kings 14 : 21–31.

The short reign of Abijam over Judah.  15 : 1–8; II Chronicles 13.
How Asa reformed the religious situation in Judah and made a
    questionable alliance against Baasha of Israel with Benhadad.
    15 : 9–24; II Chronicles 14–16.
The brief reign of Nadab over Israel.  I Kings 15 : 25–28, 31.
The vigorous reign of Baasha over Israel.  15 : 29, 30, 32–16 : 7.
The short reign of Elah over Israel.  16 : 8–14.
The reign of Zimri for one week.  16 : 15–20.

Through these minor chronicles, which reflect petty
warfare chiefly, we gain a glimpse or two of the greater
world.  Shishak of the twenty-second Egyptian dynasty boasts on his own monumental inscription at Kar-
nak of the expedition into Palestine during which he
compelled Rehoboam and others to pay heavy tribute.
In Benhadad of Damascus we take note of the firmly
established Aramean kingdom which was destined to
play an important part in Hebrew history for about
two centuries.

The three outstanding personalities were Jeroboam,
Baasha, and Asa.  Jeroboam and Baasha were devoted
to warfare and cared little for other measures.  Under
them, on the whole, Israel lost ground.  Asa was a
courageous and resolute reformer, but not, apparently,
a military genius.  He cared for his people and led the
way to prosperity as he understood it, but his measure
for obtaining peace was really an assurance of wars
(II Chronicles 16 : 9).

4.  The Vigorous Reign of Omri over Israel (I Kings
    16 : 21–28).  887–875 B. C.

The fourth consecutive Israelitish dynasty was
founded by Omri, a capable and vigorous sovereign.
Asa ruled Judah during his entire reign.  Omri brought
about great changes.  The "Moabite Stone" attests
his reconquest of Moab, which had revolted from his

predecessors. He was able to hold his own with the Arameans of Damascus. He made a useful alliance with the Phœnicians, confirming the compact by the marriage of his son, Ahab, with Jezebel, a Sidonian princess. He showed his genius as a ruler by the selection of an ideal site for a new capital, which he named Samaria. It quickly became a real rival of Jerusalem. Thus Omri, during his brief reign, gave a fresh start to Israel's fortunes. His was, however, a distinctly political genius; he was as unreligious as Jeroboam.

In his day Assyria became once more a menace to the smaller states west of the Euphrates, yet not immediately to the Hebrews. The great Ashurnazirpal (884–858 B. C.), who made the very mention of Assyria a terror, had four groups of powerful foes to deal with first. These were the Chaldeans, fairly recent settlers from southern Arabia about the head of the Persian Gulf, who added greatly to the general resourcefulness and resisting power of Babylonia; the Medes, who had begun to congregate by tribal groups in western Persia just east of the Zagros Mountains; the mountaineers of Urartu near Lake Van, persistent and formidable raiders, kept in order only by frequent expeditions; and the Aramean states of northern Syria, whose courage, strength, and skill in warfare afforded for over a century a protective barrier for Israel and Judah against Assyrian attack.

### 5. Ahab, Jehoshaphat, and Their Immediate Successors.

The remainder of the century under consideration was covered by the reigns of Ahab in Israel, and of Jehoshaphat in Judah with those of their less important successors.

THE CENTURY OF REDEDICATION   53

| JUDAH | ISRAEL | ASSYRIA |
|---|---|---|
| Jehoshaphat, 876–851 | Ahab, 875–853 | Shalmaneser III, 858– |
| Joram,[1] 851–843 | Ahaziah, 853–851 | 824 |
| Ahaziah, 843–842 | Jehoram, 851–842 | |

These thirty years or so witnessed a very active interchange between the Aramean kingdom of Damascus and the two Hebrew states. Ahab and Benhadad were repeatedly at war. Jehoshaphat entered these conflicts as an ally of Ahab and of Jehoram. Eventually Ahab met his death, and Ahaziah of Judah and Jehoram lost their lives as a result of this same warfare.

Ahab's fateful marriage with Jezebel. I Kings 16: 29–34.
Benhadad's unsuccessful campaign against Israel. 20: 1–21.
His second, severe defeat by Ahab who treated him leniently. 20: 22–34.
Ahab's denunciation for this leniency by a prophet. 20: 35–43.
The period of peace with Damascus (and the battle of Qarqar). 22: 1.
Ahab's proposal to Jehoshaphat to recapture Ramoth-gilead. 22: 2–12.
The warning of Micaiah. 22: 13–28.
The death of Ahab in the battle. 22: 29–40.
Jehoshaphat's glorious reign over Judah: his reforms, enterprise, educational activity, and prosperity. 22: 41–50; II Chron. 17–20.
His cooperation with Jehoram against Moab. II Kings 3: 4–27.
Ahaziah's brief reign over Israel. I Kings 22: 51–53.
His vain attempt to punish Elijah. II Kings 1: 1–18.
Jehoram's reign over Israel. 3: 1–3.
Joram's reign over Judah. 8: 16–24.
The joint expedition of Jehoram and Ahaziah against Ramoth-gilead. 8: 25–29.
Their death at the order of Jehu. 10: 14–28.

After Ahab had severely defeated Benhadad, he made friends with him and was his ally at the battle of Qarqar in Syria, when Shalmaneser III of Assyria, the pertinacious successor of Ashurnazirpal, won an indecisive victory. Ahab was really, as measured by his contemporaries, a wise, far-sighted sovereign. He faced great difficulties but dealt with them as a states-

[1] A shorter form of Jehoram.

man should.  He was lenient to Benhadad because he realized the value of Damascus as a barrier to Assyria's advance.  Despite his tendency to pamper himself (I Kings 18 : 42; 21 : 4) and his subservience to Jezebel, Ahab was a brave man and a wise ruler.

Jehoshaphat was much like Asa, his father.  He took his responsibilities seriously and gave his energies to the upbuilding of his people.  To the period of these sovereigns it is fair to attribute much encouragement to literature and progress of every sort.  The sense of nationalism was so strong that the origin of the fine prophetic narratives which underlie the earlier Biblical books may well be placed at this time (pp. 5, 21).

### 6. The Growth of the Prophetic Order.

An outstanding gain of this century over the one preceding was the important social and religious leadership of the prophets.  At the various crises of national life they stepped forth to remind both rulers and people of the ideals to which all should be loyal.  Many of them, of course, were members of the order as a sort of profession which would give them an easy living. Ahab maintained a troop of them, most of whom took care to give such counsel as he desired.  There were always others, like Micaiah (I Kings 22) who would not swerve from the truth as they saw it.  Some of them may have been short-sighted, but usually they were in dead earnest.  They filled an invaluable rôle in community and national life in these two Hebrew states.

They seemed to live often in communities of their own.  Doubtless they had varied pursuits.  Some were interested in following up and in recording historical or personal data.  In general they were interested in doing anything which would uphold or develop the loyalty of the people to Jehovah. Elisha was their typical leader.

## 7. The Introduction of Phœnician Baalism by Queen Jezebel and Its Promotion.

When Jezebel came to Samaria as the bride of Ahab she did no violence to any one's conscience by bringing her worship of Baal along with her. Not even an Elijah would object to that personal concession. Hence the erection of a temple to the Phœnician Baal and the importation of a body of priests may not have been in themselves offensive acts. The religious nationalism of that era assumed that each people had its god to whom it must be loyal. But Jezebel gradually threw the whole influence of the court in favor of the popular worship of her Baal. A woman every inch a queen, of great personal force, Jezebel exercised a widespread influence. On this issue she may have met with early prophetic opposition, for she had caused many to be slain (I Kings 18:13). Her heart became set upon the substitution of the Phœnician Baal for Jehovah within her adopted realm.

## 8. Elijah's Successful Championship of Jehovah and His Ways.

At this crisis, when the loyalty of the Hebrews to their God was at stake, there appeared a really great prophetic leader, who recalled them to their true allegiance. He made a mighty impression, then and ever since in world history, as a uniquely great personality. Elijah represented to his people their treasured past. He came from the wilderness and emphasized the simplicity and directness of the nomad faith. To him Jehovah was Israel's rightful God, jealous of their recognition of any other deity, protector of His people

at all times.    If they were to keep His favor they could
not serve two masters or have varying moral standards.

> Elijah appears suddenly in Israel, predicts a drought, then dis-
> appears.    I Kings 17.
> He appears to Ahab, who has sought for him in vain, to demand
> a contest with the representatives of Baalism.    18 : 1–19.
> The victorious contest at Mt. Carmel and breaking of the drought.
> 18 : 20–46.
> Elijah's flight to Horeb, where he received a threefold divine com-
> mission.    19 : 1–18.
> His call of Elisha to prophetic service.    19 : 19–21.
> His championship of popular rights against the legalized violence
> of the king.    21.
> His message of death to Ahaziah for the latter's lack of loyalty to
> Jehovah.    II Kings 1.
> His disappearance into the divine presence.    2 : 1–12.

Of these stirring stories, exhibiting a rugged, stern,
pitiless, lonely figure, those concerning the contest at
Carmel, the interview at Jezreel, and Elijah's final dis-
appearance are most important.    No greater crisis had
confronted Israel than the religious peril which drew
Elijah from his solitude.    Jezebel seemed on the very
verge of success, largely because few dared to face her
wrath or were influential enough to challenge it.    Elijah
dared to voice what many thought.    His ringing challenge on Mt. Carmel to choose between Jehovah and
Baal caused an overwhelming, impassioned response.
Yet it had to be followed up.    When the prophet fled
to Horeb, he was made to see that a campaign must be
set on foot before his task could be completed.    The
uprooting of Baalism took a generation.    Before Elijah
disappeared into the fiery symbolism of the heavenly
presence (6 : 17), he had taken two important steps.
At Jezreel he had championed popular justice, and at
Elisha's own home he had summoned him to his side as
the coadjutor who would execute the great programme.
Elisha's place in history is thus that of one who ap-

pears at an opportune moment to put in motion forces
already stirred. The prophetic order was the real rock
of popular loyalty to Jehovah.

## 9. Elisha's Completion of the Campaign against Phœnician Baalism.

The story of the career of Elisha, despite the legen-
dary element in it, pictures a forceful life, quite distinct
in its character from that of Elijah, but contributing
in its own fashion to the establishing of popular loyalty
to Jehovah.

How Elisha took Elijah's place of leadership.  II Kings 2 : 1–18.
Various instances of his dealings with people.  2 : 19–25; 4 : 1–7.
The great lady of Shunem and her experience—a picture of life in
  Israel.  4 : 8–37; 8 : 1–6.
Elisha's care for the prophets.  4 : 38–44.
The healing of Naaman the Syrian.  5.
How the prophet recovered the axe-head.  6 : 1–7.
How Jehovah protected him against the Syrians.  6 : 8–23.
The siege of Samaria and its relief.  6 : 24–7 : 20.
Elisha announces his future to Hazael.  8 : 7–15.
His anointing of Jehu as king over Israel.  9 : 1–14.
Jehu's murder of the two kings, Jehoram and Ahaziah.  9 : 15–29.
The queenly death of Jezebel.  9 : 30–37.
The destruction at Jehu's order of the house of Ahab and of the
  worshippers of Baal.  10 : 1–28.
Elisha's last act before his death.  13 : 14–21.

Elisha was clearly one who lived on intimate terms
with the people. They had implicit confidence in him.
During his long life he was able to render great services
to his country, so that the king called him its great
bulwark and defender (13 : 14). The climax of his life,
however, was the rooting out of Baalism through Jehu.
Whether he approved of the ruthless and sweeping
character of the revolution and of the reform movement, he initiated them both. In all probability he
expected bloodshed, and stopped at nothing which
would clear out of Israel the hated abomination. It is

equally probable that Jehu, once given the opportunity and impulse, executed his commission cold-bloodedly and with pitiless determination.

## 10. The Century as a Whole.

It is undeniable that during this century the Northern kingdom took the lead. It was the home and the scene of activity of the prophetic order. Under Omri it found itself, got into relationship with its world, drew into an alliance with Judah. Neither Omri nor Ahab seemed to have felt with any keenness the disloyalty to Jehovah involved in giving Jezebel freedom of initiative. The glory of blocking her purposes and forever establishing the loyalty of the people to Jehovah their God is due to the prophetic order and its great leaders. Nominally, at least, the people were always faithful thereafter to Jehovah, their God; but the bloody work of Jehu broke up the friendly relations between the two kindred peoples.

# V

## THE CENTURY OF THE GROWTH OF EACH KINGDOM TO ITS GREATEST EXTENT

### II KINGS 10 : 29–15 : 7; II CHRONICLES 22–27 (842–740 B. C.)

| JUDAH | ISRAEL |
|---|---|
| Athaliah, 842–836 | Jehu, 842–814 |
| Joash,[1] 836–796 (8) | Jehoahaz, 814–797 |
| Amaziah, 796 (8)–782 or 789 | Jehoash, 797–781 |
| Uzziah, 782 or 789–740 | Jeroboam II, 781–740 |
| (Jotham co-regent, 751–740) | |

During the next hundred years the Hebrew peoples attained the very peak of their prosperity, peace, and powerfulness. Never were they as great or as wealthy or as exultantly happy as they were about the close of the reigns of Uzziah and Jeroboam II. Yet the brilliant close of the century's experience was prefaced by a half-century of bitter, even tragic, yet rather salutary experience. Jehu's violent measures for ending the menace of Phœnician Baalism, however well intentioned, were almost as disastrous to his own dynasty and people as to those against whom he acted. Neither he nor his cousin of Judah could stand against Hazael of Damascus. But the day of Aramean supremacy passed and the Hebrew peoples prospered greatly. They thus were brought to the end of the four centuries of growth in Canaan, equipped for creative work.

## 1. The Relentless Programme of Jehu (842–814).

Jehu, chosen by Elisha to complete the desired revolution, had a soldier's view of duty. With the sanction

[1] Joash and Jehoash are really one name, used interchangeably.

of the religious leaders who were loyal to Jehovah, he
carried his programme of destruction through to the
end.  He slew the two sovereigns, Queen Jezebel, the
whole house of Ahab, and its responsible adherents,
the "brethren" of King Ahaziah, and the adherents
and leaders of Baal-worship—all in all a very great
number of important people.  It is possible that Elisha
disapproved his relentlessness, but unlikely.  Both
Elijah and Elisha had enforced such measures themselves.  It was an age of ready, unsparing bloodshed.
The participation of such a leader as Jehonadab, the
Rechabite, may warrant the inference that Jehu led a
reaction against the ruling classes which dangerously
weakened his kingdom by reducing its skilled de-
fenders.  At any rate he broke up the friendly alliance
between the two kindred peoples.

The trend of Jehu's reign.  II Kings 10 : 29–31.
Hazael's conquest of his east-Jordan lands.  10 : 32–36.

The verdict of thoughtful men in later years was
against the wisdom of Jehu's policy (Hosea 1 : 4).  It
established Jehovah's supremacy, but at a terrible national cost.  It did not really root out the pagan tendencies which permeated the life of both peoples.  No
real religious reforms can be carried through by violence.
    The worst effects of Jehu's policy did not appear un-
til after his death.  Little is said about his reign.
Jehu was evidently no such brave leader as Ahab.
When Shalmaneser III of Assyria, just at the opening
of Jehu's reign, came with an overwhelming force to
wage war against Hazael of Syria, Jehu sent Shalmaneser, as the Black Obelisk testifies, a generous tribute
in token of submission.  As a stroke of policy it was as
unwise as the earlier tribute of Asa to Benhadad.  It
gave Assyria an excuse for conquest which was never
forgotten.  Moreover, when Shalmaneser had departed,

Hazael took away from Jehu the whole east-Jordan territory north of Arnon.

## 2. New Alignments in Western Asia.

The savage and relentless policy of Ashurnazirpal (884–858), of which mention has already been made, was followed without a break by his equally famous son, Shalmaneser III (858–824 B. C.). He was an indefatigable campaigner, leading his armies for many years in person. His principal objective was the strip between the ocean and the desert from Carchemish southward. Its three principal states were Hamath, Damascus, and Israel. These, in combination with each other and with the smaller states, were able for a time to hold even Assyria in check. But Assyria attacked repeatedly; some of the allies, Jehu among them, refused to fight; Hamath was forced to submit. But Hazael determined to resist to the last. He could not expel the invader or defeat him, but he held Damascus against all assaults. Out of six campaigns the Assyrian sovereign got some territory and much plunder, but little glory. He had, however, established a policy of conquest from which his successors did not swerve.

## 3. The Dominance of Damascus over Israel.

Hazael's prompt vengeance upon Jehu for his withdrawal from the anti-Assyrian alliance was followed by a long period of humiliating oppression, during which the ruler of Damascus had Israel at his power. The result was a distressing record.

The oppression of Israel and Judah by the Syrians in the days of Joash and Jehoahaz. II Kings 13 : 1–3, 22; 12 : 17, 18.
The humiliating weakness of Israel. 13 : 7–9.
The "savior" who delivered Israel. 13 : 4–6, 23.
The reign of Jehoash over Israel. 13 : 10–13.

How the dying Elisha tried to arouse the ambition of Jehoash. 13 : 14–19.

The growing formidableness of Israel under Jehoash. 13 : 24–25; 14 : 8–14.

During the whole reign of Hazael and that of Benhadad III, his son, the Syrians were the superiors of the neighbors to the south. They not only reduced Israel in the reign of Jehoahaz to extremities, but attacked Judah with such vigor that Joash of Judah bought Hazael off with a heavy bribe. Eventually, however, an Assyrian sovereign, Adad-Nirari (810–781 B. C.), a warrior as efficient as Shalmaneser III, made three expeditions to the debatable "west-land" in the course of which he savagely attacked Damascus and greatly lowered its power. This disaster evened the strength of Damascus and Israel, so that Jehoash of Israel was able to win back some of his lost territory. Thereafter Israel steadily increased in power.

### 4. The Enthronement of Joash in Judah and His Long, Quiet Reign.

When Ahaziah was slain at Jehu's command, the haughty queen-mother, Athaliah, true daughter of Queen Jezebel, was able by reason of her great influence and her unscrupulousness to seize the throne of Judah (842–836) and hold it for six years. She tried to slay every true heir to the throne, but her own daughter, the wife of the high priest, saved the little prince Joash, then a baby, and kept him safely concealed for six years. A dramatic revolution, led by the high priest, placed Joash on the throne for a long reign, which was on the whole of value.

The rescue of the infant Joash from the murderous intent of Athaliah. II Kings 11 : 1–4.

The dramatic downfall of the usurping queen. 11 : 5–16; II Chronicles 23.

The affirmation of national loyalty to Jehovah by the people of
Judah and abolition of Phœnician Baalism. II Kings 11 : 17–20.
The proposal to repair the temple. 11 : 21–12 : 6; II Chronicles
24 : 1–5.
How Joash promoted the delayed work of repair. 12 : 7–16; II
Chronicles 24 : 6–14.
The deterioration of Joash after Jehoiada's death. II Chronicles
24 : 15–22.
Hazael's threatened attack on Jerusalem avoided by a bribe.
II Kings 12 : 17, 18; II Chronicles 24 : 23, 24.
The violent death of Joash after a long reign. II Kings 12 : 19–21.

The revolution which placed Joash on the throne of
Judah had a religious as well as a political significance.
It was a spontaneous act of the best blood of Judah.
It resulted in a solemn renewal of the national loyalty
to Jehovah, and in a rooting out of the Phœnician
Baalism which, under Athaliah's influence, had gotten
a dangerous hold upon Judah. Naturally the proposal
was made to repair the temple. The young king desired this and suggested a way of realizing the needed
funds. The priests were too absorbed by other interests to push the repairs. Finally the king himself took
charge, popular interest revived, and the work was
well and quickly done. Apparently the king's will was
supreme.

According to the Chronicler Joash deteriorated in
later life. He resented the candid criticism of Zechariah the prophet (II Chronicles 24 : 20–22), and had
him stoned to death. Hazael's attempt to capture Jerusalem quickly followed. Resentment over the read-
iness of Joash to strip the temple to buy Hazael off may
have led to his sudden murder. On the whole, however,
the reign of Joash was of value to his people of Judah.

5. The Reign of His Successor, Amaziah, over Judah.

Amaziah, like his father, had a long reign and a
rather successful one.

The reign of Amaziah like that of his father.  II Kings 14 : 1–4.
His refusal to execute clan justice.  14 : 5, 6.
His successful war with Edom.  14 : 7, 22; II Chronicles 25 : 5–13.
His challenge to Jehoash of Israel.  14 : 8–11; II Chronicles
    25 : 14–21.
How Jehoash broke down the defenses of Jerusalem and exacted a
    heavy ransom from Amaziah.  14 : 12–14.
The violent death of Amaziah.  14 : 15–20.

Amaziah promised well at the outset of his reign.
He showed excellent judgment in dealing with his
father's murderers.  His war against Edom was a sane
attempt to keep an open highway of commerce to the
port of Elath.  But general approval weakened his
judgment and led him to challenge the more redoubtable Jehoash of Israel, who so thoroughly humiliated
Amaziah that his people were alienated.  Yet his reign
as a whole prepared the way for Uzziah's success.

## 6.  The Prosperous Reigns of Uzziah over Judah and of Jeroboam II over Israel (about 780–740 B. C.).

It is one of the mysteries of sacred literature that the
next forty years, so genuinely important in the life of
each Hebrew nation, should be treated so casually by
the author of Kings.  The two kings, Uzziah and
Jeroboam II, were rulers of great ability.  Their reigns
were practically contemporaneous.  Their peoples
gained much under their leadership.  Their supremacy
was unquestioned in their areas.  Not until the very
end of the period did even Assyria begin to threaten.
Yet two formal, almost barren notices are all that were
used in Kings.

The long reign of Uzziah over Judah.  II Kings 14 : 21, 22; 15 : 1–7;
    II Chronicles 26 : 1–5.
His schemes for the safety, prosperity, and peace of his land.
    II Kings 14 : 22; II Chronicles 26 : 6–15.
How Uzziah became stricken with leprosy.  II Chronicles 26 :
    16–23.

The regency of Jotham.  II Kings 15 : 5; II Chronicles 27.
The career of Jeroboam as king of Israel.  II Kings 14 : 23-29.

In the case of Uzziah the Chronicler contributes an interesting series of facts.  He extended the boundaries of his kingdom, encouraged agriculture, protected commerce, equipped his army, and fortified Jerusalem.  It was the very sense of greatness due to these successes that led him to demand the right to share in priestly functions.  Uzziah seems to have carried to a triumphant conclusion the plans of his predecessors.  In his day Jerusalem grew rapidly in population, leadership, resources, and distinction.  It became the great city of Isaiah's active life, great alike in evils and in power for good.  For the last quarter of his reign Uzziah, stricken with leprosy, was supplanted by his son, Jotham, as regent.

Jeroboam II was a notable warrior.  He reconquered the lost east-Jordan territory, freed his people from the fear of Syria, and extended his territory clear to Hamath.  Under him Israel reached its largest area and its greatest power.  No wonder the people of Israel, as well as those of Judah, were loud in praises of their sovereigns.  The writings of the prophets, Amos, Hosea, and Isaiah furnish ample proof of their justification.

## 7.  The Significant Social and Other Changes of This Period.

The net result of these two long reigns coming at the close of an awakening century was a marked change from the older simplicity of life.  The extravagant ideals of Solomon gained great headway.  In particular the victories of each king and the established peace that followed them brought in much wealth which was not equally distributed.  The more fortunate of the people used their power thus gained oppressively. The two capitals, Jerusalem and Samaria, became centres of wealth and vulgar display. The nobles vied in building luxurious palaces. Class distinctions developed along lines of wealth. Men used their power unscrupulously to make themselves richer or more powerful, declaring at the same time, and even believing in, their fervent loyalty to each dynasty and to Jehovah, Israel's and Judah's God.

During this century the prophetic and priestly orders also seem to have attained a strength and an influence not before experienced. Since the days of Solomon the temple at Jerusalem had been under the royal control. Yet its priesthood dared to resist Uzziah's will (II Chronicles 26 : 17–19), and popular conviction went with them. An extraordinary group of prophets came to the front to voice Jehovah's protest against the evils of the day. These religious gains were paralleled by a rise in ethical tone. When Amaziah refused to subject the kinsfolk of his father's murderers to the ban he abrogated a custom of immemorial standing. To substitute individual responsibility in place of clan or family solidarity was an important step upward ethically and socially.

To this stirring century may be attributed more of the literature which is at the basis of the earlier Old Testament historical books. The prophetic narratives of early history had surely been published, likewise the narratives embodied in the Books of Judges, Samuel, and I Kings.

## 8. The Warning Voices of Amos and Hosea in the Northern Kingdom (750 B. C., onward).

Among those who viewed this frenzied life with a certain detachment and rated it at its real value were two men who were the true successors of Gad, Nathan, Micaiah, and Elijah, earnest prophets who stood ready to declare at any cost their convictions.

One of these was Amos, a farmer of Judah, who oraved the displeasure of Jeroboam and his court in order to remind the people of the Northern kingdom that, since Jehovah was essentially a righteous Being and could not in consequence condone social injustice and corruption, He would exact a reckoning from His persistently disobedient people,[1] probably through His use of the Assyrian foe, whose unchanging purpose of conquest could be safely assumed.

Not much later than Amos, and before the close of the period, another prophet, Hosea, arose in the Northern kingdom. Hosea was a cultured patriot, an ardent lover of his own country and people, yet no less clear in his characterization of the underlying evils of the day. Hosea was led through a bitter family experience to realize Jehovah's inextinguishable spirit of love. This made him more than a critic; he became an interpreter. While condemning even more powerfully than Amos the social and religious evils of the day, he yet declared that Jehovah's purpose in punishment would be not destructive but redemptive. His two great assertions of God's enduring love and redemptive purpose gave a fresh start to constructive religious thinking in an age which seemed given over to religious indifference or formalism, while the incisive declaration of Amos that God would hold His people up to His own standards of righteousness quickened a sense of social responsibility. Each prophet assumed that the Assyrian would be the Divine instrument of punishment, not that there was any immediate danger, but because

[1] For the fuller setting forth of all prophetic material see the second volume of this series, *Old Testament Prophecy.*

the Assyrian policy of conquest was well known and understood.

### 9.  The Closing Days of the Century.

Despite these warning voices, heard while Jeroboam and Uzziah were still enthroned, the last years of these two sovereigns were glorious years.   Something of the loyalty and pride of the average citizen of Jerusalem can be read between the lines of Isaiah's early utterances.   Jeroboam II maintained his ascendancy to the very end of his reign.   Measured by modern standards each country was on its way to a yet greater future. All these dreams were destined to be dissolved speedily in the face of the new Assyrian advance just gaining headway.   But the Hebrew people had now reached their topmost national development.   God could begin their real religious training.

# VI

# THE CENTURY OF VAIN RESISTANCE AGAINST ASSYRIAN AGGRESSION

## II KINGS 15 : 8–21 : 26; II CHRONICLES 27–33 (740–639 B. C.)

| JUDAH | ISRAEL | ASSYRIA |
|---|---|---|
| Jotham, 740–735 | Zechariah and Shallum, 740 | Tiglath-pileser IV, 745–727 |
| Ahaz, 735–715 (?) | | |
| Hezekiah, 715–686 | Menahem, 740–736 | Shalmaneser V, 727–722 |
| Manasseh, 686–641 | Pekahiah, 736–735 | Sargon II, 722–705 |
| Amon, 641–639 | Pekah, 735–732 | Sennacherib, 704–682 |
| | Hoshea, 732–722 | Esarhaddon, 680–668 |
| | End of Northern Kingdom | Ashurbanipal, 668–625 |

With the reappearance of able Assyrian sovereigns bent upon the conquest of all Western Asia and of Egypt, relentless and persistent in their execution of this policy, and more than ever ingenious in devising measures to make their conquests permanent, a new political programme began in western Asia which put an end to the political aspirations of the smaller sovereignties of Palestine and Syria. Judah fought for half a century before submitting to a tribute-paying status, but with the rise of the great Tiglath-pileser and his new imperialism that outcome was more or less inevitable. Assyria's overwhelming prowess affected the development and the destinies of the Hebrew people so deeply that the middle of the eighth century may be counted as a third great turning-point in Hebrew history, comparable with the entrance into Canaan and the disruption of Solomon's kingdom.

69

At this time the real test of the preceding four centuries of organized religious growth took place. The Hebrew peoples were threatened with absorption into the Assyrian empire. They naturally relied upon Jehovah for protection and multiplied their devotedness to Him. This situation enabled the four prophets of the half century following 750 B. C.[1] to reinterpret God's character and demands in moral and spiritual terms rather than in terms of sacrificial worship. They pointed out the sins of the people and Jehovah's probable use of the Assyrian invader to awaken the public conscience. They appealed for a loyalty to God which would transform lives and affirmed a certain future on such a basis. Thus was a political tragedy converted into a means of spiritual and moral uplift, and of national assurance. It was a real miracle.

1. **Tiglath-pileser IV and His Policy of Conquest (745–727 B. C.).**

During the reigns of Uzziah and Jeroboam II three relatively weak sovereigns occupied the throne of Assyria. They gave no concern to the people of distant parts. But about 746 B. C. there arose, perhaps out of humble origin, one of the greatest military monarchs of early history, Tiglath-pileser IV. He was not only a military genius but an administrator of unusual capacity. Not content to ravage a country and lay it under heavy tribute, Tiglath-pileser instituted a regular policy of the deportation of the most aggressive portion of its population, settling alien peoples, often from the Assyrian homeland, in the abandoned districts. Thus he hoped to prevent rebellions and gradually to unify the empire.

This redoubtable leader gave his earliest attention

[1] See *Old Testament Prophecy*, p. 27.

to Babylonia and to the countries east and north of Assyria. In 742 B. C. he was free to deal with Arpad and other Aramean states. Two years later Arpad was conquered, a signal for the prompt appearance of gifts of friendship from the little states to the south. About four years later his campaigning against these peoples began, and brought about the formation of a formidable coalition of nineteen states, including Northern Israel, to resist Assyrian demands. Had this alliance held together under trusted and competent leadership, even Tiglath-pileser might have been defied. One of the first to yield when the Assyrian army appeared in south Syria was Menahem of Israel (II Kings 15 : 19, 20). He paid a heavy ransom and submitted. Thereupon Tiglath-pileser conquered the other members of the coalition one by one, added all northern Syria to the territory of his empire, applied his policy of deportation and colonization extensively, and went back to his capital at last triumphant. The ultimate doom of Damascus, Samaria, and Jerusalem was clear.

2. The Situation in Palestine as Interpreted by Prophetic Minds.

The prophet Hosea was probably active during the disquieting years of Tiglath-pileser's advances into Syria and Palestine. Isaiah of Jerusalem, too, as a young man just beginning his prophetic career, was a keen observer of his strategy. To each mind the Assyrian became the expression and instrument of Divine displeasure with His people. Jehovah was going to permit the foreign invader to attack Palestine, not because He was impotent, but because no other measure seemed adequate to rouse the Hebrew peoples from their self-satisfaction, selfishness, and absorption in unrighteous aims and to quicken their conscience. These prophets justified the Divine action by giving it a moral meaning.

Hosea quite despaired of his own people. They had gone too far. He had the bitter experience of seeing the Northern kingdom go rapidly down to certain ruin. At best he could put his faith in God's love, which would be persistently redemptive. Isaiah, on the other hand, could take, at the outset of his prophetic career, a less despairing view. His consistent advice to Ahaz was to keep faith with Jehovah and to have faith in Him.

### 3.  The Dramatically Rapid Downfall of the Northern Kingdom (740–722 B. C.).

At the end of Jeroboam II's reign Israel seemed secure, yet in eighteen years it went to ruin. During that short time there were six rulers and four changes of dynasty. Internal strife, foreign invasion, and crushing tribute each contributed to the social and political chaos which prevailed.

The six months' reign of Zechariah. II Kings 15 : 8–12.
Shallum's conspiracy and briefer reign.  15 : 10, 13–15.
Menahem's submission to Tiglath-pileser.  15 : 14, 16–22.
Pekahiah's brief reign.  15 : 23–26.
Pekah's loss of territory to Tiglath-pileser.  15 : 25, 27–31.
Hoshea's revolt and appeal to Egypt; the siege and capture of Samaria.  17 : 1–6; 18 : 9–12.
An editorial review of the history of northern Israel.  17 : 7–23.
How the imperial policy of deportation altered the religious character of the population.  17 : 6, 24–41.

Of the six sovereigns of Israel after Jeroboam II four were murdered, one died in prison, one only died a natural death. Menahem, Pekah, and Hoshea deserve brief mention. Both Menahem and Pekah had to bear the brunt of Assyrian attack. In one case the kingdom was drained of money; in the other much territory was lost. In 732, two years after the annexation of the Galilee and east-Jordan country, Tiglath-pileser crushed Damascus and absorbed it. This left only central Palestine, Samaria proper, under the rule of Pekah, with the accessible plain of Esdraelon· his northern boundary. Pekah was slain by Hoshea, who, under the patronage of Assyria, succeeded him on the throne of Israel. But we may well assume that Hoshea's attempt to secure the aid of Egypt was a counsel of utter despair. His action gave Shalmaneser V, who succeeded Tiglath-pileser, a good excuse for annexing Israel. The strong city of Samaria was not to be captured with the weapons of that day, but starvation compelled its final capitulation 722 B. C. The leading citizens were deported; their places were filled by the new Assyrian sovereign, Sargon, with subjects from other lands; an Assyrian governor was placed over the new province or district of the empire. The northern Israelitish kingdom was no more.

### 4. The Historical Place of the Northern Kingdom.

The Northern kingdom existed for a little over two hundred years. It started with many advantages. Its policy was unfettered by precedent; it had a fertile country, abundant population, and relatively ample resources. During the two centuries, however, it suffered eight changes of dynasty. No steady process of development was feasible. Israel's brilliant genius manifested itself in flashes rather than through a steady flame. The losses overbalanced the gains. Yet in its free, nationalistic atmosphere the prophet seemed to flourish. It could boast of many noble men and women. The "great lady" of Shunem was no doubt a type of its gracious and fair women. Its leadership, while erratic, was real. Israel set the pace in many ways, literary, economic, social, and religious, for Judah. This was fortunate, since Judah, while less originative, was better fitted to preserve and protect whatever progress was gained. The downfall of Israel did not cause a loss of the good things for which she had stood.

## 5. The Reign of Jotham and Ahaz over Judah.

Jotham is credited in II Kings 15 : 33 with a reign of sixteen years, but no such period is available between the death of Uzziah and the early years of Ahaz. We know, however, that Uzziah was afflicted with leprosy, perhaps for many years. During this period Jotham acted as regent. If these years were credited to him as regnal years, then his own separate reign was rather brief. At all events Ahaz was on the throne by 735 B. C. During his reign one fatal step was taken over the protest of Isaiah.

> The reign of Jotham over Judah. II Kings 15: 5, 32–38; II Chronicles 27.
> The religious tendencies of Ahaz. 16 : 1–4; II Chronicles 28 : 1–4.
> The alliance of Rezon and Pekah against him. II Kings 16 : 5; Isaiah 7 : 1–2; II Chronicles 28 : 5–15.
> Isaiah's advice to have faith in Jehovah's care. Isaiah 7 : 3–9.
> Ahaz's submission to Tiglath-pileser. II Kings 16 : 7–9; II Chronicles 28 : 16, 20, 21.
> His relations with surrounding peoples. II Kings 16 : 6; II Chronicles 28 : 17–19.
> His imitation of Assyrian religious customs. II Kings 16 : 10–20.

Very little can be said about Jotham's reign apart from that of Uzziah. He doubtless was responsible for much of its halo of success. According to the Chronicler he, like his father, was a successful and prudent warrior, amassing wealth through tribute.

When Ahaz came to the throne of Judah, Pekah had seized Israel's crown. The next three years were fateful. Rezon of Damascus and Pekah sought to organize an alliance of the smaller states to resist the anticipated demands of Tiglath-pileser IV. Into this alliance Ahaz refused to go. Whether he acted from statesmanlike or cowardly motives is not readily answered. Rezon and Pekah determined to compel him to join them and moved against him. Isaiah tried hard to induce Ahaz to ignore them and to put his faith in Jehovah. Ahaz preferred to curry favor with Tiglath-pileser, and submitted to him, paying a generous tribute. He thus saved his people from immediate and future invasion, but paid a heavy price. By his act Judah became a tributary to Assyria.

Ahaz found much to admire among the Assyrians. He had a new great altar made after the pattern of one he saw at Damascus, and put it into constant use at the temple, relegating that of Solomon's to subordinate use. Probably his attitude opened the way for the introduction of the Assyrian religious practices which prevailed later (II Kings 23 : 11, 12).

To pass judgment on Ahaz is not easy. Some regard him as a weakling, buying protection at the cost of honor. Possibly his policy was one of deliberately cynical opportunism, successful in that it saved his state from the disasters which wrecked so many others, yet unapproved by such brave and sagacious leaders as Isaiah.

### 6. The Character and Policy of Hezekiah.

In 715 Hezekiah succeeded to the throne, a young but very promising man. He was greatly influenced by Isaiah. During his reign a real reformation took place, which re-established firmly the worship of Jehovah.

The reformation of Hezekiah and his warfare with the Philistines. II Kings 18 : 1–8; II Chronicles 29–31.

How Isaiah blocked one revolt against Sargon.  Isaiah 20.
The severe illness of the king and the visit of Merodach-baladan's
  envoy.  II Kings 20 : 1–19.

Hezekiah had evidently the qualities of leadership. He was the sovereign of greatest importance and resourcefulness in Palestine. Other peoples rallied around him. Yet no small element in his stability and power was the support and advice of the prophet Isaiah, in whose wisdom both king and people had great confidence. When Egypt's promises of support led Ashdod to revolt, Isaiah was able to deter his own people from following its example. That Hezekiah was not exempt from the vanity which is natural to kings was shown by his dealings with the messengers of Merodach-baladan, king of Babylonia, which Isaiah rebuked so plainly and severely. Yet, by and large, he was a noble and righteous sovereign.

## 7. The Great Crisis During Sennacherib's Invasion of Palestine.

Sargon of Assyria died in 705 B. C. and was succeeded by Sennacherib, a man of blood and iron. His subject peoples very generally revolted. Those in Palestine were again stirred by Egypt into a concerted revolt which no satire of Isaiah's about "Madame Brag and Sit-Still" (Isaiah 30 : 7) could prevent Judah from joining. He pleaded in vain that they rely upon Jehovah's aid. A very strong pro-Egyptian party was formed, headed, apparently, by Shebna the prime minister. Isaiah was strong enough to secure his dismissal from his exalted post and to promote a change of royal policy. During the exciting months that followed Isaiah was the trusted adviser of Hezekiah.

Sennacherib's first approach: Hezekiah's submission.  II Kings
  18 : 13–16; II Chronicles 32 : 1–8.

Isaiah's opposition to an alliance against Sennacherib. Isaiah
18 : 1–19 : 17; 28–32.[1]
Sennacherib's later attempts to force a surrender of Jerusalem.
II Kings 18 : 17–19: 34; Isaiah 36; 37; II Chronicles 32 : 9–23,
32, 33.
His sudden departure to Assyria. II Kings 19 : 35–37.

In 701 Sennacherib was ready to attend to his subjects in Palestine. He advanced from Assyria swiftly
with a huge force. Phœnicia, Philistia, and Egypt in
turn were defeated. He then turned to Judah, laying
it waste and besieging Hezekiah in Jerusalem. Realizing the hopelessness of the situation Hezekiah paid a
heavy tribute for raising the siege. Later, Sennacherib
demanded the absolute surrender of the city, a gross
breach of faith on his part, as well as a challenge to the
popular reliance on Jehovah. But Isaiah did not quail.
At this time of crisis he was calm, resolute, and sure.
The issue was Jehovah's; Isaiah dared to declare that
He would vindicate His character and preserve His own
city. Evidently Sennacherib tried twice to capture
Jerusalem. The latter attempt may have been some
years later. But the city never had to surrender.
Isaiah's contention that it was Jehovah's inviolable
sanctuary seemed publicly justified. The deliverance
made a lasting impression on the people of Judah.

The closing years of Hezekiah's reign must have
been happy years, fruitful in much that makes a people
great. But Assyria had shown her overwhelming power.
Judah was now a vassal state, paying regular tribute.
What this would mean for national hopes had yet to
be determined. Such a current prophecy as that of
Isaiah 2 : 2–4 and Micah 4 : 1–5 seems to indicate a
calm confidence in a real future.

[1] For a careful analysis of Isaiah's prophetic utterances, see the second volume in
this series, *Old Testament Prophecy*, p. 23ff.

## 8. Manasseh's Long Reign over Judah (686–641 B. C.).

With the accession of Manasseh, the young son of Hezekiah, to the throne a reaction took place. The innate heathenism of Jerusalem (Ezekiel 16 : 3), long repressed but never wholly extirpated, asserted itself under the patronage of the court with irresistible force, and became highly popular. The Assyrian customs introduced under Ahaz became the fashion. The prophetic adherents, even with such leadership as Isaiah's, were soon in real peril. Its members had to hide away. According to tradition Isaiah was murdered. The result of this sudden change from public leadership to popular hatred forced a great but not unsalutary change of prophetic methods.

Early in Manasseh's reign Sennacherib was succeeded by Esarhaddon, an energetic, reasonable ruler (680–668), who was followed, in turn, by the greatest Assyrian sovereign of all, Ashurbanipal, still at the height of his power when Manasseh died.

The religious innovations of Manasseh. II Kings 21 : 1–9; II Chronicles 33 : 1–9.
The prophetic view of his reign. II Kings 21 : 10–15.
His discipline. II Chronicles 33 : 10–13.
His royal career. II Kings 21 : 16–18; II Chronicles 33 : 14–20.

The reign of Manasseh, viewed from any other angle than that of religion, was one which contributed its share of advance. Judah was avowedly a tributary to Assyria, but the relationship assured peace and the restoration of prosperity through trade within the wide-ranging empire which, under Esarhaddon, included Egypt. Moreover, the influence of a friendly Assyria was distinctly cultural. It is generally assumed that the Babylonian calendar was adopted by the Hebrews at this time. Religiously the movement was more for

absolute freedom than against the recognition of Jehovah.   It was the exclusiveness of the prophets which
caused such hostility to them.

The withdrawal of the prophets from public appear-
ances gave a great impetus to literary advance.   Writing was the only efficient method of appeal open to
them.   The actual productiveness in literature of the
half century we may only conjecture.   It seems probable that much was done by way of collecting and editing the sermons of the four prophets of the earlier half
of the century, and by way of revising and extending
the covenant law to fit the new prophetic ideals.   Proverbs 25 : 1 argues for still other sorts of literary activity.

## 9.   The Century as a Whole.

The one hundred years of Hebrew history which followed the reigns of Uzziah and Jeroboam made significant changes in Hebrew life.   The Northern kingdom
came to an end, not ingloriously, yet decisively.   What
it had embodied in custom or prophetic appeals lived
on.   Judah became a vassal nation, yet succeeded in
maintaining a reasonable freedom.   The nation suffered severely from war, yet gradually recovered a
greater prosperity than before.   For a half century it
put prophetic ideals of religion under the ban, but
thereby stimulated a literary activity which gave a new
outlet to prophetic teaching and a new breadth to
its programme of reform.

# VII

## JUDAH'S CLOSING HALF CENTURY : A PERIOD OF GRADUAL POLITICAL DECLINE

### II KINGS 21 : 19–25 : 21; II CHRONICLES 34–36 (639–586 B. C.)

| JUDAH | ASSYRIA |
|---|---|
| Josiah, 639–608 | Ashurbanipal, 668–625 |
| Jehoahaz, 608 | Ashur-etil-ili ⎱ 625–606 |
| Jehoiakim, 608–597 | Sin-shar-ishkun ⎰ |
| Jehoiachin, 597 | Capture of Nineveh, 606 |
| Zedekiah, 597–586 | CHALDEA |
| | Nabopolassar, 625–604 |
| | Nebuchadrezzar, 604–562 |

The reign of Amon, the son of Manasseh, was un-
eventful and brief. A palace conspiracy brought it to
a sudden close. A popular movement, which reflected
a long-impending desire for a change in public policy,
placed Amon's infant son, Josiah (639–608 B. C.), on
the throne of Judah. The little king was under the
care of a group of wise and loyal guardians, whose influence gave promise of a speedy restoration of the traditional strength of the kingdom. Prophetic ideals
once more gained ascendancy in shaping the currents
of national life, outstanding evils were abated, and an
era of prosperity ensued. That these results were not
permanent was due to a fateful combination of causes
which will appear in the narrative. In spite of them
Josiah's reign left its own ineffaceable and salutary
stamp upon the national life.

The last quarter century before the Exile was a period of steady national decline, yet one of glorious spiritual achievement. Such a king as Jehoiakim was a curse to Judah, but such minds as those of Jeremiah, Habakkuk, and Ezekiel were its salvation. Jeremiah in particular, because of his very loneliness and bitterness of life, made Divine discoveries which enriched the world for all time.[1] Ezekiel, made an exile, discovered that he could move the hearts of his fellow captives to sanity and serenity of soul.

1. **The Young King and His Advisers (639–621 B. C.).**
Josiah was eight years old when he ascended the throne. According to the Chronicler, he repeatedly manifested a marked interest in religious reforms before he attained his twentieth year, but the record of Kings and the prophetic data converge upon the years following 626 as being the truly important years of his rule. So far as the evidence goes, Josiah was a faithful tributary of the great Assyrian sovereign, Ashurbanipal (668–625 B. C.), whose closing years bore lightly upon the subject peoples of his vast empire, and gave them increasing internal freedom.

The great Assyrian empire was, in fact, nearing its end. The policy of expatriation had been carried so far that there was no longer a reliable, homogeneous, absolutely loyal central state available for terrorizing the world. The unity of the empire depended upon the personality of its sovereign, who had become old and pleasure-loving. Its weakness was demonstrated by the inroads of the fierce Scythians who came pouring out of the north to ravage the empire. These hordes on horseback could not attack with any success walled cities, but they ravaged at will the lands through

[1] See *Old Testament Prophecy*, pp. 36, 43.

which they wandered.  Herodotus tells us that they
followed the coast as far as the border of Egypt, but
were turned away by Psamtik I.  Jerusalem and Judah
they seem to have left untouched, but the menace of
their presence seems reflected in Zephaniah and in
Jeremiah 2–6.

The brief reign of Amon over Judah.  II Kings 21 : 19–26; II
Chronicles 33 : 21–25.
Josiah's first eighteen years upon the throne.  II Kings 22 : 1, 2;
II Chronicles 34 : 1–7.
Josiah's reliable advisers.  II Kings 22 : 3, 4, 12, 14; Zephaniah
1 : 1; Jeremiah 1 : 2.

Two prophets shared definitely in the shaping of the
royal purpose and in the preparation of the public
mind during this period, Zephaniah and Jeremiah,
each coming to public notice about 626 B. C.  One
had royal blood in his veins; the other came from an
old, influential priestly stock.  Zephaniah's austere
message of immediate and genuine repentance on pain
of Jehovah's sweeping judgment was balanced and supported by Jeremiah's tender yet vigorous appeals to
Judah to be loyal to the nobler ideals of the past (Jeremiah 2–6).  Together they quickened the conscience
of the nation regarding its religious obligations.[1]

## 2.  Josiah's Project of Repairing the Temple and Its Startling Outcome (621 B. C.).

Notwithstanding the attitude of the young king and
the vigorous appeals of these prophets, supported
surely by the prophetic party among the people and
by the officers of the king's cabinet, the work of reform
might have been more difficult, if the death of Ashurbanipal and the accession of a feeble successor had not

[1] See *Old Testament Prophecy*, pp. 31, 32.

given Josiah an unusual degree of freedom of action. Of this he took full advantage.

> Josiah's measures for the repair of the temple.  II Kings 22 : 3–7; II Chronicles 34 : 8–13.
> The discovery of the "book of the law."  II Kings 22 : 8–11; II Chronicles 34 : 14–19.
> Its confirmation as authoritative by Huldah, the prophetess.  II Kings 22 : 12–20; II Chronicles 34 : 20–28.
> Its public reading followed by a popular acceptance of its provisions. II Kings 23 : 1–3; II Chronicles 34 : 29–32.

Josiah's programme of reform began at the temple. During the many decades of neglect it had come to be in sore need of repair.  II Kings 22 : 4, 7 indicates the fine spirit in which the people entered upon the sacred task.  It was progressing happily when Hilkiah, the high priest, made a great discovery.  He found a book, a law code, which impressed him and Shaphan so greatly that they took it directly to the young king.  It was evidently a surprise to the king and to his advisory circle.  The prophetess, Huldah, was consulted regarding its genuineness.  Receiving her sanction the young king took immediate steps to have the code publicly read.  It made a profound impression upon all and at once received general acceptance as a code which should govern the life of Judah.

## 3.  The " Book of the Law " and the Movement for Reform.

This code of law which affected courtiers, king, and people so strikingly, must have been short enough to be read aloud easily, and must have contained exhortations, warnings, and promises as well as legal material.  Without doubt it was substantially what we know to-day as the book of Deuteronomy, at least the legal portion of it, chapters 12–28.  The code embodied in this book exactly corresponds to the reforms which were carried out. Why it had been laid away, and why King Josiah's circle was unacquainted with it are questions which can only be answered by conjecture. The most probable view of its origin is that the Deuteronomic code was the result of the application of the prophetic ideals of Amos, Hosea, Isaiah, and Micah to the religious and social regulations obtaining in the eighth century. It was a reformulation of the established Mosaic law to make it express the new conceptions of Jehovah, of national life, and of individual character and responsibility. These ideas make the greater part of the difference between it and the covenant code, Exodus 20 : 23–23 : 19, which, as already pointed out (p. 27), was probably the social code of the earlier kingdoms. The Deuteronomic code made one marked change in the religious procedure of the people. It centralized all sacrificial worship at Jerusalem. It served as the accepted basis of social and religious life for the next two hundred years.

Josiah's abolition of the altars and symbols of Canaanite or Assyrian worship in Jerusalem. II Kings 23 : 4–14; II Chr. 34 : 33.
His abolition of the altars of sacrifice and of unworthy practices throughout the land. II Kings 23 : 15–20, 24.
The great passover celebration. II Kings 23 : 21–22; II Chronicles 35 : 1–11.
The compiler's comment. II Kings 23 : 25–27.

The reform that followed the adoption of the new law was sweeping indeed. A wave of moral enthusiasm swept over the land. The temple and capital city with their surroundings were cleansed of the altars and symbols of the forms of worship that had been encouraged by Manasseh. All other sanctuaries than Jerusalem were defiled, their priests being slain or brought to Jerusalem for service. The reform was as thorough-going as such a reform can ever be. It overrode all opposition. Not only King Josiah and his officers, but such leaders as Jeremiah (11 : 1–8), supported the movement.

4. **The Remainder of Josiah's Reign (621–608 B. C.).**
The next twelve years was a period of great outward prosperity. Josiah was a patriotic, noble-minded ruler. His people increased in numbers and resources. Very probably Josiah added to his dominion a part of the old Northern kingdom. Could he have had a longer reign or have had a successor like himself, the little kingdom might have had a fresh lease of life.

But world conditions were changing rapidly. The Assyrian empire which had endured for over a thousand years and had led its world for half that time, now, sadly weakened, was facing its end. Its last king was no weakling, but he ascended the throne too late to save it. The new empire of Chaldea and the confederation of the Medes joined forces against Assyria and doomed it to extinction. Several years before Nineveh was actually captured the prophet Nahum foretold its downfall.[1]   Pharaoh Necho II, of Egypt, an able, ambitious, and aggressive ruler, saw his opportunity to regain some of Egypt's long-lost domain, and to become a great Asiatic power. In 609 he marched with a great army toward the Euphrates. Gaza and Ashkelon were readily taken; other cities offered no resistance. His way seemed clear and easy until Josiah of Judah interposed.

The vain attempt of Josiah to block Necho's advance. II Kings 23 : 28–30; II Chronicles 35 : 20–24.
The universal lamentation over Josiah's death. II Chronicles 35 : 24, 25.

[1] See *Old Testament Prophecy*, p. 35.

The popular choice of Jehoahaz (Shallum) as king. II Kings 23 : 30.
Necho's reversal of this choice and selection of Jehoiakim.   II
    Kings 23 : 33, 34; II Chronicles 36 : 1–4.

We well may wonder at Josiah's boldness.  He paid
a great price for the freedom he would continue to enjoy.  His little army met that of Necho at Megiddo
and was decisively routed, the king losing his life.
Thus came to a sad and sudden close a life of promise,
and Judah became subject to Egypt.

By a species of popular vote Jehoahaz, a younger
son of Josiah, was made king of Judah.  This choice
was later overruled by Necho, who summoned the
newly chosen king to Riblah, in Syria, where a permanent camp had been pitched.  There Jehoahaz was
treated with every mark of indignity, his older brother
Eliakim was placed on the throne under the royal name
of Jehoiakim, and Judah was heavily fined.  Evidently Jehoahaz and those who chose him were regarded as hostile to Egypt.  He was taken to Egypt
as a prisoner and soon died, as Jeremiah had foreseen
(Jeremiah 22 : 10–12).

### 5.  The Early Reign of Jehoiakim (608–601 B. C.).

The first years of Jehoiakim's reign were full of stirring world events.  The actual capture of Nineveh
by the Medes and its destruction took place in 606
B. C.  In the partition of the Assyrian empire the
Chaldeans took the territory lying west of the Tigris.
The first great issue to be decided by Nabopolassar,
their king, was the question of supremacy on the coast.
He sent his son, Nebuchadrezzar, with an army to meet
Necho's vast host at Carchemish, where he inflicted a
crushing blow to Egyptian ambition.  The Egyptian
army fled in confusion to Egypt, followed by the vic-
torious prince.  The sudden news of his father's death

compelled Nebuchadrezzar to abandon the pursuit and
to hasten to Babylon, but not before Syria and Palestine had submitted to Chaldean rule.

Jehoiakim's first three regnal years. II Kings 24 : 1.
Jeremiah's reference to the overthrow of Necho. Jeremiah 46 :
2–12.
Habakkuk's study of the place of the Chaldean in God's universe.
Habakkuk 1, 2.

For the first seven years of his reign Jehoiakim was
loyal, first to his Egyptian overlord, then to Nebuchadrezzar.  At least he paid tribute.  Each overlord
had a heavy hand.  The prophet Habakkuk reflected
the mind of many a righteous soul when he asked how
Jehoiakim could permit so inhuman and greedy a nation as the Chaldean to control the destinies of his
own people?  Jeremiah explained the Chaldean overlordship as Jehovah's challenge to his unrepentant
people (Jeremiah 25 : 1–14).  These seven years had
been sad ones for the prophet.  Jehoiakim hated him:
all classes therefore ostracized him.  He found his way
and his work blocked.  These experiences drove him,
however, continually closer to God and gave him
fresh prophetic visions.[1]  He was the great man of his
age.

There developed in Judah a party of patriots who
were eager to renounce allegiance to Nebuchadrezzar.
So far as the Biblical evidence goes, the only strong
voice raised in opposition to this foolish proposal was
that of Jeremiah.  But his opposition only helped the
cause of the enthusiasts, who were probably given
secret encouragement from Egypt.  In 601 the annual
tribute was refused.

[1] For the instructive details of this interesting and creative prophetic period, as
revealed in the writings of Jeremiah, see *Old Testament Prophecy*, pp. 35–47.

## 6. The First Capture of Jerusalem and First Captivity (601–597 B. C.).

Nebuchadrezzar did not immediately invade Judah, either because he belittled the revolt or because he was occupied at home with momentous matters. He ordered such Chaldean soldiery as were available, together with auxiliaries from Syria, Moab, and Ammon, to make forages in Judah. Such guerilla warfare, however, had little effect. In 597 the great king was ready to act.

The guerilla warfare against Jehoiakim.  II Kings 24 : 2.
The editor's explanation of the situation.  24 : 3, 4 (compare Jeremiah 22 : 13–19; 12 : 7–17; 13 : 15–27).
The sudden death of Jehoiakim.  II Kings 24 : 5, 6.[1]
The brief reign of his son, Jehoiachin.  24 : 8, 9.
The surrender of Jerusalem and first captivity.  24 : 10–16.

Nebuchadrezzar with his army quickly invested the city. At or just before this crisis Jehoiakim died, leaving the throne to his son Jehoiachin, who occupied it nominally three months. There was no hope of succor. Hence the young king with his mother and court surrendered unconditionally, before any assault of the city took place.

Nebuchadrezzar dealt with the people of Judah in a way which he probably regarded as merciful. He carried away to Babylon the royal family, the court, the important leaders, seven thousand fighting men, and a thousand handicraftsmen. These were the choicest section of the people, the "good figs" (Jeremiah 24 : 2–5), the natural leaders. All these with their families were settled in Babylonia on the banks of the Chebar, one of the huge, river-like canals, where they were permitted to live their own community life. The conqueror took away some temple treasures (II Kings

---

[1] The statement of II Chronicles 36 : 6 lacks confirmation.

24 : 13; Jeremiah 27 : 19), yet left the land and city essentially untouched.

## 7. Zedekiah's Helpless Reign (597–586 B. C.).

Nebuchadrezzar placed on the throne of Judah a third son of Josiah, Mattaniah, giving him the regnal name of Zedekiah. The new king was quite young. His intentions may have been good, but he could not cope with the situation. He respected Jeremiah, but could not protect him. He was surrounded by inexperienced, headstrong advisers who disregarded past experience in a passionate, blind patriotism, which trusted, in spite of Jeremiah's bold declarations, that Jehovah would not permit the Chaldean king to destroy Jerusalem, His abode.

The exact sequence of events is uncertain, yet apparently the first half and more of Zedekiah's reign was passed without outward disloyalty. Jeremiah was active in counselling the captives in Babylonia to settle down in expectation of a long stay (Jeremiah 29 : 4–14), and in denouncing the false prophets at home whose counsel was so harmful (23). But a strong party existed, both in Babylonia and in Judah, which believed that patriotism meant anti-Chaldeanism. It heard Jeremiah with impatience. When he declared his conviction that the yoke of Nebuchadrezzar was unbreakable, and that submission to him was the only dictate of wisdom for any people (Jeremiah 27 : 5–11), the prophet Hananiah dared to break the yoke with which Jeremiah had been symbolizing his plea, declaring "Even so," saith Jehovah, "will I break the yoke of Nebuchadrezzar, king of Babylon, within two full years from off the neck of all the nations" (28 : 11). These were strenuous days. Jeremiah might, however, have won, since after 592 B. C. he had the vigorous support of another great prophet, Ezekiel, whose messages uttered by the Chebar were quickly known in Jerusalem.

But a new factor entered into the situation. In 588 B. C. a new king, Hophra, arose in Egypt, able, ambitious, and crafty. He lost no time in promising to assist the little peoples of Palestine to defy Nebuchadrezzar. They promptly revolted. No influence could restrain Judah from entering this movement. Both Jeremiah and Ezekiel denounced the revolt as an act of treachery to Jehovah Himself, but to no purpose.

Zedekiah made king of Judah. II Kings 24 : 17–20.
How Jeremiah tried to prevent rebellion. Jeremiah 27, 28, 29.
The long siege of Jerusalem by the Chaldeans. II Kings 25 : 1–2.
Their temporary withdrawal to meet the advancing Egyptians; what befell Jeremiah. Jeremiah 34, 37, 38.
The capture of the city and of the king. II Kings 25 : 3–6.
The sweeping judgments inflicted by Nebuchadrezzar. 25 : 6–21.
Gedaliah made governor of Palestine and his fate. 25 : 22–26.

By the end of the year a Chaldean army appeared before the walls of Jerusalem. The city was a real fortress of great strength, capable of withstanding a long siege. It could not be taken by direct assault, so the great army invested it and settled down to starve it into submission. The Hebrews were grimly determined to hold out to the last. They had hopes of relief from Hophra. That sovereign did, in fact, lead an army into Palestine. The Chaldean forces raised the siege in order to meet this force.

Great were the rejoicings of the people in Jerusalem. Many among the wealthy who had freed their slaves at the request of King Zedekiah and in token of repentance now compelled them to render their old obedience (Jeremiah 34 : 8–22). Only Jeremiah was unchanged. He warned the people that the Chaldeans had not gone permanently. He was hated as a traitor. Attempting to leave the city at this crisis on some private business, he was suspected of a desire to desert, was beaten, and then thrust into prison. From this he was rescued only to be cast into a waterless cistern, lest his continual advising of the people to surrender should weaken the defense. Only the friendly aid of a negro eunuch of the palace preserved the prophet's life (Jeremiah 37, 38).

## 8. The Final Capture and Destruction of Jerusalem (586 B. C.).

Having driven the Egyptian army back into Egypt, the Chaldeans once more invested Jerusalem closely. Famine and probably pestilence weakened the defense. Eventually a break was made in the walls, and the eager army poured into the doomed city. Zedekiah fled away at night, but was pursued, captured in the plains of Jericho, and carried off to Riblah, where Nebuchadrezzar dealt with him ruthlessly. Meanwhile Jerusalem was plundered, sacked, and laid in ruins. The long resistance of its people had so enraged the Chaldeans that they deliberately laid waste the city and its surroundings. They proposed to end forever the defiant state. The peasantry out in the country parts, such as were left, were not carried away, but a second captivity, chosen as before from the richest and most representative among the inhabitants, was carried away to Babylonia.

## 9. The Four Centuries of National Life.

About four hundred years had elapsed since the rise of nationalism under David. Half of the period was required for laying a proper foundation of experience and development. The less than two centuries from the days of Amos and Isaiah, Uzziah and Hezekiah, had been Israel's golden age, when her leaders were

awakening to the real significance of the Divine leadership of the nation.  Although the Hebrew nationality seemed to have been crushed by the brutal
strength of the Chaldean, the real Hebrew life was un-
affected.  In fact, as we shall see, it was set free!  The
Hebrew people had developed ideals that were now to
gain a universal recognition.  They were ready to enter upon a new and vastly important phase of their
wonderful history.

One of the first and most valuable results of this new
life was the impulse given to literary production.  Not
only were the early prophetical narratives of the beginnings of Hebrew history (pp. 5, 21, 54, 66) combined
with the Deuteronomic code into an enlarged "Bible,"
but the records of the centuries following the Conquest
were edited into the present books of Judges, Samuel,
and Kings (pp. 24, 46, 72), while the current prophetical and other literature was brought up to date.

# VIII

## THE BABYLONIAN EXILE

### (586–538 B. C.)

CHALDEA
Nebuchadrezzar, 604–562
Amil-Marduk, 561–560
Nergal-shar-usur, 559–555
Labashi-Marduk, 556
Nabunai'd (Nabonidus), 556–538

With the destruction of Jerusalem and the transfer
of the most influential section of the Hebrew people to
Babylonia, we reach the fourth great turning-point in
Hebrew history. The crossing of the Jordan, the disruption of David's kingdom, and the entrance of Assyria into world politics, each was the occasion of a
radical change in the life of the Hebrew people. Of
equal importance with the first-named was the Babylonian exile. It marked four sweeping changes in Hebrew life. The people came to be generally known as
Jews ("Judeans"); they exchanged landowning and
agriculture for commercial pursuits; they became a cosmopolitan people who could make their home anywhere; most of all they dropped idolatry and made religion a primary interest of life. They felt that their
exile was a grievous punishment for their sins. They
came in time to see that Jehovah had enabled them to
make it a wonderful opportunity.

During this half century they not only learned a
new type of living and acquired a culture hitherto un-
familiar, but they also gained through their great pro-

phetic leaders both a supreme conception of religion and its significance and a fresh idea of the value of religious organization. From many angles these fifty years were all-important in Hebrew development. They brought to a climax the vigorous religious thinking of two centuries, declaring that Jehovah was the one God of the universe, and defining religion in terms of missionary obligation.

## 1. The Exiled People.

Jeremiah had declared that the exile would continue for seventy years (Jeremiah 29 : 10). Evidently this was a round number, but it was not far from correct. A full half century passed before a Jew could lawfully return to the city of his hopes and prayers. During this period the captives lived such relatively free lives in Babylonia and elsewhere that they insensibly made the new environment their natural one. Never again did the bulk of the people live in Palestine; they became internationalized.

Nebuchadrezzar had left the weakest but probably most numerous section of the original people as peasantry in Palestine; another strong group was in Egypt, composed of those who had fled thither from time to time; the portion in Babylonia, possibly the least in numbers, was by far the most representative of the best Jewish blood. It carried the destinies of the people with it.

## 2. Ezekiel's Task and How He Performed It.

When the second group of exiled families reached Babylonia, both they and those who had preceded them by a dozen years were wholly disheartened. Despite the warnings of Jeremiah and Ezekiel they had believed that Jehovah would protect His people, city, and temple. But now their dynasty was broken, the temple and city in ruins, the priesthood without means of worship. The very foundations of their life seemed to have given away. They could only call themselves "dried up bones" (Ezekiel 37 : 11). The "Lamentations" express the depths of their woe. Had not such noble leaders as Ezekiel been at hand, they could with difficulty have renewed their hopefulness and taken a forward look.

Ezekiel set himself to the task of enabling his downhearted people to get a fresh grip on life, and to settle down to await patiently the better days ahead. Jeremiah had remained in Judah for a similar purpose, but had been carried away to Egypt. Some fifteen years of earnest, pastoral service are represented by Ezekiel 33–37. The prophet set forth the loving sympathy and abounding goodness of Jehovah, His tenderness and patience with His sinful people, and proclaimed that while He had been forced by His people's sinfulness to discipline them, the future could yet be bright. He could readily make a new and powerful nation even out of dry bones (Ezekiel 37 : 3–6). Ezekiel's encouraging words gave new life and hope to the exiled community. But he was also an organizer. In a striking vision of the future temple and its services (40–48) he embodied a scheme which so clearly indicated how the Israel of the future could function that it actually readjusted the religious policy of the Jewish people. His genius foreshadowed the Judaism that was to be.

### 3. The New Life in Babylonia.

The new life in Babylonia was many-sided. The Jews were not greatly restricted except in their freedom to return to Judah. They entered freely and with success into the commercial opportunities of their new home. They utilized its educational advantages. They were impressed by its learning, its strength, and its resources. To what degree they mingled socially with the haughty Chaldeans is uncertain. Apparently their most representative men, like Daniel, were on friendly terms with the court. In great measure, however, the Jews maintained their own exclusive society and carefully preserved their own ways of life and thought (Jeremiah 29 : 5-6). Religiously they made a great discovery which fitted into the assertions of Jeremiah and Ezekiel. They found it possible to be truly religious in spirit and obedient to Jehovah although no longer able to offer sacrifice to Him at Jerusalem. They formed the habit of meeting in groups for prophetic counsel, for prayer, and for the reading of the writings of their revered leaders. Thus the synagogue as a social and religious institution came into being. It so approved itself that it became permanent. A good-sized group of religious leaders, especially priests, busied themselves in collecting, codifying, and adjusting the ritual laws which had been in use, but had not been put into written form. Some of these at least appeared eventually in the Holiness Code (Leviticus 17-26). Ezekiel's programme of worship in the temple-to-be (40-48) gave evidence of the influence of this legal activity. The ideas which the people were ready to adopt were not merely those of olden time, but such ideas adapted to current needs.

The fortunes of the people left by Nebuchadrezzar in Palestine and of the prophet Jeremiah. Jeremiah 40-43.

Ezekiel's helpful ministry to the Babylonian group of exiles. Ezekiel 33-37; 40-48.

The friendliness shown to the imprisoned Jehoiachin by the son of Nebuchadrezzar on his accession. II Kings 25 : 27-30.

## 4. The Fortunes of the Chaldean Empire.

The reign of Nebuchadrezzar covered the first half of the exile. He had made Babylon a synonym of world power, even Egypt being helpless before him. He had consolidated, organized and held a vast empire. He wished posterity to judge him by his reconstruction of Babylon, the city of his heart. Its huge walls were completed, the streets were reconstructed, the royal palace rebuilt, the temples restored, the great canals made secure. Thus a great, beautiful, impregnable city developed, on which he well could gaze with pride (Daniel 4 : 30). At the same time he made similar restorations and rebuildings all over the empire. Of these undertakings rather than of his successes in war his numerous inscriptions tell the story. He truly sought to serve his people and his gods. He left no real successor.

His son, Amil-Marduk (Evil-Merodach), succeeded Nebuchadrezzar (561–560 B. C.). The one Biblical fact about him is that he set free the hapless Jehoiachin, who had been in prison some thirty-six years, recognizing his royal standing. After a reign of two years he was slain. His successor, Nergal-shar-usur, had a brief though vigorous reign of four years. His young son, Labashi-Marduk, reigned less than a year. In 556 B. C. a conspiracy of nobles and priests placed Nabuna'id, the last Chaldean ruler, on the throne, which he occupied for seventeen years. This rapid succession of rulers was disastrous to the Chaldean empire. There was no commanding personality to wield the full power of the throne. Nabuna'id was far superior to these predecessors, yet he was a man of scholarly tastes, an antiquarian, who spent his time and resources in the discovery and renewal of ancient temples and in honoring their gods, rather than as an administrative sover-

eign. The actual management of his empire he left to
the crown prince, Belshazzar.

## 5. The Rise of Cyrus the Persian.

Under ordinary circumstances the empire might still
have endured for a generation or more, since its great
rival in power, Media, cared little for universal dominion. About 550 B. C. three rulers, Nabuna'id, the
Chaldean; Astyages, the Mede; and Crœsus, the Lyd-
ian, controlled between them the western half of all
Asia. Then a new personality suddenly challenged
that world. Cyrus, the prince of Anshan, defeated
Astyages, his overlord, and within three years had over-
whelmed Crœsus and conquered all of Asia Minor.
Cyrus built a solid foundation for the Persian empire
by uniting all the tribes and peoples who before had
been loosely confederated. By 546 B. C., therefore, the
western Asiatic powers were reduced to two in number.

For several years Cyrus made no serious attempt to
invade the dominions of Nabuna'id. That he would
do so ultimately was perfectly apparent. To this time
of crisis one may quite safely attribute such voices as
those of Isaiah 21 : 1–10; 13 : 1–14 : 23; and 44 : 24–
47 : 15, which were declaring the impending fate of
Babylon and the plans of God; and, probably, the
wonderful declarations of Isaiah 40–55 which reached
the very peak of prophetic insight, explaining the past
centuries as a time of training and the coming task as
that of evangelizing the world.[1]

In 539 B. C. Cyrus was ready to advance. He
reached Babylon after slight opposition and entered its
gates through priestly treachery without striking a
blow. Belshazzar, the co-regent, was slain, and Na-

[1] See *Old Testament Prophecy*, pp. 53–58.

buna'id was deported. Thus at a stroke all western Asia passed from the rule of the Semite to that of the Aryan and a new chapter of human progress began. The first effect was startling. A very prompt decree of Cyrus was one encouraging the captive peoples in Babylonia to return to their homelands with all their goods, there to rebuild their old prosperity and to enjoy their own type of life in their own way. No wonder it was said of him that he ruled whole peoples as successfully as the good householder ruled his family.

## 6. The Results of the Fifty Years of Exile.

This half century had wrought great changes in the Hebrew people. For the majority Babylon had become a relatively desirable home. It was emphatically the land of individual opportunity, both economic and cultural. Their sojourn had not lessened the hold of their religion upon them, but it had broken the spell of Jerusalem and of Judah. Henceforth the home of the greater part of Jewry was the world. Wherever business opportunity beckoned, they made themselves at home. To many a loyal Jew this indifference to Judah as a home seemed a matter to be challenged and overcome. But it was all in the Divine plan to have it so. The "Israel abroad" was relatively more useful in spreading lofty religious idealism over the world than those who lived in Palestine. Neither could be spared: each had its share in the work of preparing the world for Christ. Both had reason to be thankful for the two generations spent by the people in Babylonia.

# IX

## THE BUILDING OF THE SECOND TEMPLE

### EZRA 1–6 (538–516 B. C.)

| THE JUDEAN RULERS | | PERSIAN KINGS |
|---|---|---|
| Zerubbabel, the prince | 538–516 | Cyrus, 538–529 |
| Joshua, the high priest | or later. | Cambyses, 529–522 |
| | | Darius, 521–485 |

The generous permission of Cyrus for the return of the captive Jews of Babylonia to their Judean homeland and for the rebuilding of the temple and city did not draw out a corresponding response from the Jews who were his subjects. In place of a general departure to Judah only a small band returned. The great king exercised no compulsion: he left the decision to the Jews themselves. But a half century of unrestricted community life in Babylonia had created new ties. Babylon seemed like home to the great majority of the people. Most of those who had actually lived in Judah were dead. Only deep-seated and very genuine religious zeal would carry men and women back to wasted Judah, abandoning Babylonian opportunities.

The work achieved in Judah during the next two decades was due to the zeal and constancy and foresight of a relatively small group of choice Jews. They were able to see that at all hazards Jerusalem must once more be the acknowledged religious centre of the Jewish people. This implied the rebuilding of the city and of the temple. The latter task was within their resources at the time. How deeply spiritual was the purpose of the best among them is to be inferred from

100

the glorious preaching of the prophet Zechariah.[1]  He was such another leader as Jeremiah or the Great Unknown.

## 1. The Return of a Group of Exiles to Judah.

The story of the return as given in Ezra 1–4 contains perplexing data, on the proper interpretation of which students sharply disagree.  It is clear, however, that a loyal band was organized in 537 B. C. to make the long journey to Jerusalem.  The listed thousands of Ezra 2 may represent the muster roll of citizens in the days of Nehemiah nearly a century later (Nehemiah 7). The real group was probably much smaller, but it was a choice group.  Joshua the priest and Zerubbabel, a prince royal, headed the volunteers.  The first governor appointed by Cyrus may have been Sheshbazzar (1 : 8;  5 : 14–16), but, at any rate, Zerubbabel was his successor.

The friendly proclamation of Cyrus.  Ezra 1 : 1–4.
Freewill offerings in aid of the return to Judah.  1 : 5–11.
The muster roll of those who (eventually) migrated.  2 : 1–70.
The speedy building of the altar at Jerusalem.  3 : 1–7.
The public laying of the cornerstone of the second temple.  3 : 8–13.
The exclusion of the "people of the land" from the task of building and their reaction.  4 : 1–5, 24.

On reaching the goal of their hopes the pilgrims were eager to establish a regular altar service on the sacred hilltop.  They repaired the altar, observed the feast of Tabernacles and such other feasts as were due, and inaugurated a simple but regular system of worship. With overpowering joy they thus renewed the religious experiences of the past.

[1] *Old Testament Prophecy*, pp. 59–65.

## 2. Plans for Rebuilding the Temple.

According to the book of Ezra, they lost no time in taking steps to rebuild the temple. Workmen were secured and timber engaged from the Phœnician merchants. Early in the second year they laid the foundation stone with due ceremony. It was with mingled joy and grief that aged and strong alike saw the apparent fruition of their long-cherished hopes. The "people of the land," probably those who were in large part of Jewish blood but who had deteriorated during the half century and were not recognized by the Babylonian leaders as worthy to represent Jewish ideals, asked for a share in the enterprise. When rather curtly refused, they became bitter enemies, blocking the transport of timber and otherwise preventing the continuance of the task. For sixteen years this situation continued.[1]

## 3. The Accession of Darius to the Throne of Persia.

Cyrus died in 529 B. C., leaving a united and prosperous realm. His son, Cambyses, lacked the father's gift for government and for self-control. He added Egypt to the empire over which he ruled, but he could not develop it properly. He took his own life in a fit of rage on hearing that a pretender to his throne was making headway during his absence in Egypt. This rival, Smerdis, impersonated a younger brother whom Cambyses had slain secretly. Smerdis was slain by a group of suspicious nobles, who elected one of their own number, Darius, to the throne of Persia. Not being an heir to the throne, Darius had to face and master a revolt in each one of the great provinces of

[1] The full historicity of these interesting details is open to question, although they must rest on real tradition. Some students, on the authority of I Esdras, transfer these achievements to the early reign of Darius.

the Persian empire. This great task he had achieved by the early months of 519 B. C.

## 4. The Appeals of Haggai and Zechariah on Behalf of the Temple.

Meanwhile, either during the interval of relaxed supervision in the "westland," or because something encouraging had happened, two prophets of the Judean colony seized the opportunity to recall the community to its duty. It had made no attempt to press the building of the temple, yet its members had made comfortable provision for themselves. Haggai and Zechariah felt that the hindrances were no longer serious and that concerted action could achieve the desired and important result. They set themselves to the task of arousing their people. Haggai led off with a trumpet-like appeal to "arise and build," following this exhortation with others at frequent intervals.

The successful appeal of Haggai and of Zechariah to the people to build the temple. Ezra 5:1, 2. *Cf.* also Haggai and Zechariah 1–8.

The inquiry of Tattenai, the governor of the province, and its happy outcome. 5:3–6:13.

The completion of the temple in the sixth year of Darius. 6:14–15.

The solemn dedication of the new temple. 6:16–22.

The effect was magical. With fresh heart the people entered into the sacred task. The prophet Zechariah not only added his influence to Haggai's, but during the four years of building did much to emphasize the significant relationship of the temple to the religious future of the people.

It was not at all strange that the governor of the great Persian province of "Beyond-River" (*i. e.*, west of the Euphrates) should hear of the unusual activity in Jerusalem and inquire into it. The Jewish community is reported to have cited the decree of Cyrus as their justification. When this was reported to Darius, the decree was found, whereupon the great king not only confirmed its terms, but ordered the governor to aid the people in speeding up the work. Under such royal approval the temple rapidly reached its completion in 516 B. C., the sixth year of Darius, and was dedicated with great solemnity.

### 5.  The Significance of the Temple.

In size and general arrangement the new temple was probably much like the old one. Most of the costly equipment and adornments which Solomon provided had disappeared. The new temple must have been in comparison with the old rather plain and unimposing, yet it had even greater dignity. It stood alone on Mt. Zion. No royal palace shared its impressiveness; no hint of the civil power belittled its importance. It embodied, in accordance with Ezekiel's vision, the unchallenged dominance of God, and exerted an influence which far exceeded that of its predecessor.

The vast majority of all those of Jewish blood lived outside of Palestine, but the new temple caused great rejoicing among them. It was the symbol of their religion, the visible goal of their hopes. It meant to them that Jehovah once more dwelt with His people, and that His promises were surely to be fulfilled in His good time. It defined and steadied their loyalty; because of the Temple and its meaning Jerusalem became the rallying and standardizing influence in Jewish life.

### 6.  The Disappearance of Zerubbabel.

Haggai, Zechariah, and the Jerusalem community had set high hopes upon Zerubbabel, the prince. They

looked to him to fulfil the prophetic promises of ideal
leadership. Zechariah specifically regarded him as
answering Jeremiah's prediction (Jeremiah 23 : 5) of a
"Branch" (Zechariah 3 : 8). But they were doomed
to disappointment. Zerubbabel disappeared from view
in the course of the long reign of Darius (521–485 B. C.),
and with him the Davidic dynastic hopes. Either his
rule was lacking in success, or it led to some intrigue,
or else the centralizing policy of Darius caused the
gradual setting aside of influential local leaders. To
the Jews in Palestine and to Jews everywhere this must
have been deeply disheartening. There was no prophet
great enough to comprehend the real method through
which God was to execute His purposes. Not through
any political supremacy of the Jewish community in
Judah, however devoted that group might show itself
to be, but through the infiltration of the world of that
day by little Jewish groups who went wherever business
opportunity opened, was the world to be drawn toward
higher religious ideals. The leadership for which all
loyal Jews longed was not to be through the sort of
king they anticipated. For the Divine purpose the
Israel abroad became of greater importance than the
Israel at home. This was not realized, however, until
one more great step had been taken by those at home.

## 7.  The New " Israel."

The completion of the temple concluded the period
of exile. With its dedication the old life was resumed,
yet with a fresh and stronger setting. The seventy
years of Babylonian influence had wrought several important permanent changes in the religious life of the
Jewish people. The old temptation to idolatry seems
to have disappeared. All devotion centered about
Jehovah and the temple at Jerusalem. The old dis-

tractions had ceased to have any power. There was no king who thought of the temple and its belongings as being subject to his will. The supreme national authority in the community was the high priest, especially after the civil headship passed to a foreigner. As the people realized their political impotence, the whole trend of popular activity and interest became religious. The synagogue and the scribes grew in importance and influence along with the priesthood and their Levitical associates. The worship at the Temple gave an incentive to psalmody that produced many of the beautiful hymns of our Psalter.

Four changes in religious thinking and practice began to be evident: (1) Under the influence of such leaders as Ezekiel there was a marked increase in the ritualization of religion. (2) Babylonian and Persian thought may account for a growing sense of Jehovah's greatness and distance from His people. (3) This remoteness of Jehovah made easier the current recognition of superhuman beings who were His intermediaries (Zechariah 1:9, 13; 2:3; 3:5). (4) Most marked of all was the gradual transition in religious thinking from the prophetic view-point which stressed the duty of the individual to the apocalyptical hopes which expected Jehovah to fulfil His promises through the exercise of His overwhelming might. In any case, however, men's minds rested on God. Religion had become to them the supreme fact in history. They were in line to become the world's teachers about religion.

# X

## THE FIRM ESTABLISHMENT OF JUDAISM

EZRA 7 : 1–NEHEMIAH 13 : 31 (516 TO ABOUT 330 B. C.)

| PERSIAN KINGS | GREEK RULERS |
|---|---|
| Darius, 521–486 | Philip, 359–336 |
| Xerxes I, 486–466 | Alexander, 336–323 |
| Artaxerxes I, 466–425 | |
| Darius II, 425–404 | |
| Artaxerxes II (Mnemon), 404–358 | |
| Artaxerxes III (Ochus), 358–337 | |
| Darius III, 337–331 | |

The century and more which followed the rebuilding
of the temple was a period during which the tendencies
already noted toward formalism, organization, and authority in religion came slowly to fruition. There is
no reference in the books of Ezra or Nehemiah to the
first sixty or seventy years of this time. There are
sound reasons, however, for concluding that the lot of
the Judean community was not prosperous, perhaps
deplorable. Not only did the Messianic expectations
fail to materialize, but the community seemed pursued
by ill fortune. Harvests failed, yet the tax-gatherer
was merciless. The priesthood became careless and
even corrupt. Social injustice led to scepticism and
thus to indifference to exactness of ritual, to regularity
of temple worship, and even to racial purity. There
was real danger of a breakdown all along the line of
racial distinctiveness, when the prophet Malachi and
Isaiah 56–66 entered their glowing and earnest appeals
for reform. It is fair to say that the proper main-

tenance of these ideals waited upon the rebuilding of
Jerusalem as a secure city with a wall and a policy.
Nehemiah's work undergirded reform in the only sure
way. He was, like Ezra, a coadjutor of these prophets.

## 1. The Persian Empire and the Greeks.

These unrecorded decades were years during which
the Persian empire was at its best. Darius was a firm,
just, and skilful ruler. He adopted a provincial organization of his vast empire that enabled him to control it absolutely. He introduced coined money into
Asia, made Persia a power on the sea as well as on the
land, and built excellent roads all over the empire.
His one thorn in the flesh were his Ionian subjects, who
gave him much trouble, being assisted by the Greeks
of Europe. He determined to subjugate the whole
Hellenic peninsula. A huge army and fleet in 492 B. C.
met with disaster. Another greater army was defeated
at Marathon. In the midst of his preparations for a
third expedition Darius died. His son and successor,
Xerxes I (486–466 B. C.), determined at all costs to
crush the defiant opponents of his will. He raised an
enormous array and fleet which he accompanied in
order to witness their prowess. At Salamis the huge
fleet was routed by that of Athens. The next year at
Platæa the Persian army was scattered and compelled
to flee. No Persian army ever invaded European soil
again. Moreover, the Greeks had learned their power
and henceforth were ready to take the aggressive in
Asia. They could do little for over a century, for they
were not united, while the Persian empire was colossal
in size and in resources. For the next thirty years,
until well into the reign of Artaxerxes I (466–425 B. C.),
the gradual decadence of the Persian empire was
hardly noticeable. This last-mentioned sovereign was

the friend and patron of Nehemiah, whom he enabled to render a supremely important service to the Jewish race.

## 2. The Data Regarding Nehemiah and Ezra.

The data regarding the work of Nehemiah and of Ezra are found in Ezra 4: 8–23; 7–10 and in Nehemiah. These data were assembled by the writer of Chronicles, who lived over two hundred years later than the events. They seem in great confusion, and concerning their interpretation there is a strong difference of opinion among competent students. The order, as outlined below, is discussed later.

The evils which came to prevail in the Jerusalem community. Isaiah 59 : 1–8; Malachi 1 : 7–10, 13; 2 : 10–11; 3 : 8.

How Ezra the scribe obtained permission to lead an expedition from Babylon to Jerusalem. Ezra 7.

The departure from Babylonia and safe arrival at Jerusalem. 8.

Ezra's decisive action in regard to mixed marriages. 9, 10.

An attempt to build the wall of the city frustrated. 4 : 8–23.

The delegation from Jerusalem appeals to Nehemiah at Susa. Nehemiah 1 : 1–3.

His resolve to undertake the task of rebuilding Jerusalem. 1 : 4–11.

His successful plea to Artaxerxes and appointment as governor. 2 : 1–8.

His shrewd preliminary study of the situation at Jerusalem. 2 : 9–16.

His successful appeal to the whole community to join in the enterprise. 2 : 17–3 : 32.

The various stratagems of Sanballat and his group to block the work on the wall. 4 : 1–23; 6 : 1–14, 17–19.

The measures taken by Nehemiah to redress the wrongs of the weak and poor in the community. 5 : 1–13.

His own self-sacrificing generosity to all. 5 : 14–19.

The noteworthy completion of the city wall. 6 : 15, 16.

The measures taken to guard the city against attack. 7 : 1–4.

Those taken to increase the population of the city. 11 : 1, 2.

The solemn dedication of the walls. 12 : 27–43.

Nehemiah's second visit and vigorous reforms. 13 : 4–31.

The public reading of the Law under Ezra's direction. 8 : 1–12.

The proper celebration of the feast of Tabernacles. 8 : 13–18.

The public fast and confession of sinfulness.  9.
The solemn covenant to obey the Law.  10:1-29.
Its obligations.  10:30-39.

The events described in these chapters may cover
the latter half of the fifth century B. C.  That they
took place may be regarded as certain; the order in
which they happened is obscure.  Many thoughtful
students hold that Nehemiah preceded Ezra.  Some
hold that the Artaxerxes under whose patronage Ezra
made the journey to Jerusalem was not Artaxerxes I,
Nehemiah's patron, but Artaxerxes II (Mnemon), who
reigned from 404-358 B. C.  Some go so far as to regard Ezra as the mere personification of the historical
trend toward the reorganization of the religious life of
the Jewish people which was conceived and developed
by the scribes.  Allowing liberally for the idealizing
tendencies of the Chronicles, this conclusion seems un-
warranted and unnecessary.  Some such leadership as
that of Ezra seems as essential to the remarkable
achievement of establishing Judaism as the social and
religious guide of the Jewish people as that of Nehemiah
was needed for the rehabilitation of Jerusalem and the
community.  We may, therefore, properly regard him
as a historical character and study the records, not
alone to furnish a clear account of the two great achievements, but as portraying two typical leaders, who did
much for the Jewish people.

### 3.  The Situation Which They Faced.

The situation which initiated this important half
century is vividly set forth in the prophetic writings
which are to be dated about the middle of the fifth century, Isaiah 56-59, 63-66 and Malachi.[1]  Each reveals

[1] See *Old Testament Prophecy*, pp. 66-71.

a deplorable situation, socially and religiously. The priesthood, who wielded authority, had grown very lax. They tolerated intermarriage with surrounding peoples, probably for the sake of the commercial and social advantages involved. They permitted and exhibited indifference in regard to worship. The Sabbath was neglected. The wealthy oppressed the poor. In brief, the community was rapidly losing its morale and was in danger of losing such religious uplift as it had gained through the re-established temple.

Whether Ezra or Nehemiah was the first to deal with this situation will always remain a matter of dispute. The Chronicler, by the order of his narrative, implies that the priority was with Ezra. Since, if this was the case, the reader must conclude that Ezra's reforms were so sudden and sweeping that they brought about a reaction which set him aside for thirteen years, it will afford a clearer view of the half century and its changes to begin with the rehabilitation of Jerusalem under Nehemiah, about 445–430 B. C. The story of his enterprise, told largely in his own words, is one of the fascinating narratives of the Old Testament. Evidently the Chronicler adopted Nehemiah's own, first-hand memoirs.

### 4. Nehemiah's Summons to Service.

Conditions at Jerusalem had never been satisfactory since the first return under Joshua and Zerubbabel and the building of the temple. Much of the city still lay in ruins. It lay open to hostile attack. Its walls had never been repaired. Ezra 4: 8–23 relates an attempt to do this, which was ended by force, possibly not long before the appeal to Nehemiah. In despair the better citizens determined to turn for aid to their countryman, Nehemiah, and sent a delegation on the long journey

to Susa to give their appeal due emphasis.  Nehemiah
was a favorite of Artaxerxes, his personal cupbearer,
influential, wealthy, and cultured, one of the foremost
men of his race.  It is not strange that the community
at Jerusalem determined to place its case before such
a man, a loyal, important and friendly-minded Jew.
Nehemiah might well have said that he could not yield
his influential place at the heart of the empire for the
task of reconstructing a little community, but he was
no ordinary man.  He realized even better than the
deputation the importance of the task in the light of
world-wide Judaism and its future.  Dedicating himself to it prayerfully, he waited the opportunity to gain
the requisite permission from his sovereign.  When it
came he was prepared to ask for what he needed.
He was made governor of the district with ample
powers.

### 5.  Nehemiah the Builder.

The Jewish community had many enemies who were
profiting by its weakness and had no desire to see its
security.  They had been able, hitherto, to baffle all
real attempts to make the city and community strong.
In Nehemiah they encountered an opponent of a new
order.  He was the great king's friend; he had the
authority of a ruler; he was a man of fine training and
of varied experience.  When he reached Jerusalem his
first act was to see the situation for himself, his second
to unite the people for an enthusiastic, cooperative rebuilding of the walls of the city.  He guarded them at
the work and dealt with all opposition, some of which
was exceedingly clever.  Nehemiah was too genuine
and too wise to be entangled by his opponents; he kept
the work going so that in a very short time the wall of
the city was repaired.

## 6. Nehemiah as Organizer and Reformer.

During the preceding century few Judeans had lived within the confines of the ruined city. The bulk of the Jews who made the temple the centre of their religious life lived in the villages round about. Many of these were persuaded to take up their abode in Jerusalem. The city was quickly made secure also through proper organization. Nehemiah then held a solemn festival of dedication in which the leaders participated, marking the importance of what had been done.

Nehemiah grappled boldly with the situation in the community. At a great people's assembly he charged the grasping men of property with sinful unbrotherliness in their treatment of the poor, and forced them, through very shame, to reform. He set all a noble example of a friendly and generous use of power. During his second governorship, after a short interval at court, he put through with vigor a series of religious reforms which he may have left previously to the priesthood. He regulated the distribution of the Levitical tithes; he expelled foreign intruders, he forced the proper observance of the Sabbath and insisted on the discontinuance of the habit of marrying Gentiles. A chief offender was the grandson of the high priest, who had married a daughter of Sanballat, the Samaritan chief. Nehemiah expelled him from the community.[1] These vigorous measures went far to unify and hearten the community. It began to live up to its principles.

## 7. The Importance of Nehemiah's Work.

The value of Nehemiah's contributions to the life of his people can hardly be overestimated. First of all, he embodied in his own fine personality the good traits of his people at their best—lofty patriotism, far-sighted-

[1] He was instrumental in establishing in Samaria, a parallel religious practice, which persists even to-day.

ness, efficiency, the spiritual view-point, and entire devotion to the execution of his principles. He bettered the community by his mere presence. Then he carried to completion the task of making it secure. He built more than a wall : he recreated a racial life. Judah had to be at its best in order that all the Jews who looked to Jerusalem should maintain their standards. Finally Nehemiah insisted that those standards, already clearly defined, should be loyally sustained. He was in full sympathy with the ideals of Jewish life as they had been formulated during a century or more by devoted leaders. Without his leadership these would have been in danger of lapsing at the sacred city itself.

## 8. The Task of Ezra.

On the foundations which Nehemiah thus laid there were others eager and ready to build. For several generations the Jewish scribes, whose headquarters had remained in Babylonia, had been at the work of codifying the whole law. The Deuteronomic code, adopted 621 B. C. (p. 84) and recognized as the standard law of the Jewish people, was a social more than a ceremonial code. But Ezekiel and those who followed him had urged the importance of a fresh emphasis upon ceremonial in the interests of holiness. The scribes, therefore, gave themselves to the congenial task of collating all the established ceremonial usages, of formulating and codifying them. The outcome was the elaborated code found in the books of Exodus, Leviticus, and Numbers, generally known as the Priestly Code, which, as noted earlier (p. 96), incorporated the earlier and simpler codes. The extent of genuine editorial work cannot be clearly defined. The code was an aggregation of groups of ceremonial legislation, developed over a period of several centuries, formulating on the whole an elaborate ritual for the guidance of life, socially as well as religiously, religious demands being counted as supreme in importance. Like the Deuteronomic code it was truly Mosaic in principles.

Ezra, the scribe, assumed the duty of securing the free adoption of this comprehensive ceremonial law by the people at Jerusalem as the standard law of community life. There are those who regard Ezra as only the personification of a slow, irresistible movement toward a ceremonial system extending over many years. The question is relatively unimportant, since no one questions the actual adoption of the new system within the range of the fifth century. In favor of the narrative as given in the Bible it may be urged that the actual putting into play of any such far-reaching changes would surely have called for the persistent advocacy of some such leader as Ezra, whose failings are those common to geniuses of the study, but whose energy, devotedness, and greatness of soul are unquestioned.

## 9. His Mixed Marriage Reform.

Ezra 7–10, which tells the story of Ezra's going from Babylonia to Jerusalem, represents him as a famous scribe who yearned to secure the adoption at the holy city of the scheme of strict religious and social life which he and his brethren had worked out. He secured permission from Artaxerxes to head a new pilgrimage, gaining many unusual privileges. In either 458 or 397 B. C. (according to the Artaxerxes of Ezra 7), he reached Jerusalem with a numerous train of devoted men and women, and with costly gifts for the temple. Soon after his arrival he learned that the people of the Jewish community, abetted and even led by those whose example should have been corrective, were permitting marriages with the surrounding peoples, and thus endangering the purity of the Jewish stock. Ezra felt acutely the danger of this course and took measures to stir the popular conscience. They urged him to take proper steps to set the situation right. He thereupon appointed a commission of inspection which in three months carried through a drastic reform, compelling those who had married foreign women to put them away. Whether this was judicious or not, it was effectual. Public sentiment became prevailingly antiforeign thereafter.

### 10. The Adoption of the Ceremonial Law.

The greater task before Ezra was the adoption of the new law by the community (Nehemiah 8–10). At a time not exactly to be determined, either soon after the reconstruction of the city by Nehemiah or long afterward, the whole community assembled to hear the law which Ezra had brought. All were in a receptive mood, of which Ezra took full advantage. For hours he read aloud the book of the Law, his associates interpreting the Hebrew into Aramaic, the language which the people spoke. The hearts of all were deeply moved; a spirit of glad obedience prevailed. Day after day the public reading continued. The outcome was a solemn rededication of the whole people to the service of God and the signing of a covenant, through their representatives, that all would live by the provisions of the new law. The covenant explicitly mentioned (1) the avoidance of marriage with those of alien blood; (2) the rigid observance of the Sabbath; (3) the observance of the sabbatical year; and (4) the regular provision of supplies, so that the temple service could be maintained with full dignity and completeness. Thus came to fruitage the long, patient, persevering work of the scribal order, which had welded into a workable unity the ceremonial usages of the centuries since Moses.

## 11. The Character of This Law.

Through this law thus adopted officially at the centre of Jewish life the ritualistic tendencies of Jewish religious life reached a climax. The idea emphasized by Ezekiel and in the Holiness code (p. 96) that the holiness of the people could be best upheld by a rigid ceremonialism which should control the whole active life of the people was put into actual practice. The nation became a church, its purity carefully guarded from outside contamination by rigid rules, its aim the earning of forgiveness for sins, its one great anxiety the exact execution of every religious or ceremonial duty. Such a type of religious life was something new in Israel's history. Neither the original Mosaic measures, nor the covenant legislation, nor the Deuteronomic law, nor the historical data found in the books of Samuel and Kings reflect it. It was a fresh working out of the underlying Mosaic principles into a scheme of life which recognized Jehovah as the Lord of all, which made His proper worship life's supreme obligation, which found its highest joy in doing His will, which emphasized afresh the uniqueness of Israel's place in His plans for the world and gave it the task of perfect obedience and worthiness. This Priestly Code, as students term it, was the expression of a noble idea. Its great defect was that it formulated duty in terms of ceremonial rather than in terms of character and spiritual aspiration. It did not overlook the latter elements, but assumed their development under the system. The prophetic emphasis was on the moral and spiritual point of view as being eternally important. It valued ceremonial as an adjunct to religious life, not as its chief expression.

## 12. Its Gradual Establishment.

Judaism seemed to express and satisfy the religious needs of that day. It seems to us to have replaced the noble idealism of the prophets by a formal institutionalism which made religion an irksome daily task. But obedience to the Law, however complicated, was cheerfully assumed; the round of religious duties kept alive in the hearts of most Jews a real religious spirit. It is generally agreed that only the close organization of Judaism enabled it to survive the fierce conflicts and fiery trials of the centuries immediately following. The Jews not only became adjusted to their religion as shaped by the requirements of the Law, but this standardization of their every-day life brought them both joy and strength. The Pharisaism and the Rabbinic developments of later days were really one-sided outgrowths.

## 13. The Priestly History.

Among the scribes of priestly origin were some who felt the need of another history of their people. They did not undervalue, necessarily, the combined prophetic history and law book which represented to their generation the interpretation of that history, and of its ideals by venerated pre-exilic prophetic minds (p. 92). They felt, however, that a history was needed which should explain the origin and value of Israel's peculiar institutions, now become so important in their eyes, yet overlooked in large measure by the prophetic historians, and they set themselves to the task of preparing it.

This history began with the stately poem about creation of Genesis 1, whose sublime conception of God in His creative power seems much more akin to Isaiah 40–48 than to earlier thinking. It upheld throughout the idea of a holy Sovereign, supreme in majesty, sitting in judgment on men. Yet it dwelt distinctively upon the details of descent, upon the origins of sacred customs and ritual practices, and upon the growth of a sense of covenant relationship between Israel and Jehovah. As a history it contributed little to the data already known; but it set forth a truly religious explanation of the organized growth of the nation.

## 14. The Hexateuch.

Early in the fourth century B. C. the last step in the literary growth of the first six books of the Bible, as we know them now, must have been taken, the combination of the priestly history and the priestly legislation with the prophetic histories and the Deuteronomic legislation. Each was highly valued by the people as sacred literature. On the basis of the priestly outline of history the scribes fitted in the prophetical material, making only the most necessary adjustments. Hence the careful reader of the Hexateuch finds it to be a curious mosaic of varied material, some primitive, some matured. It is not a uniformly written narrative of events from the creation to the days of the judges, but a collection of data, historical, religious, legal. It reflects all stages of religious growth and appeals to all kinds of religious need. When read with its strange literary history in mind, the Hexateuch stands out as a wonderful achievement, amply justifying the verdict of a unity wrought out of remarkable variety.

## 15. The Character and Significance of Judaism.

The substitution of ritualism for religious spontaneity replaced the disorders of the earlier religious life by a systematized worship marked by dignity, impressiveness, and purity. Judaism became, however, more than a machine-like scheme of regularity in worship directed by an elaborate ecclesiastical organization. It was a body of enlightened thinking about God and the world which put forth a steady current of religious idealism, so well organized and maintained by habitual practices that it could challenge successfully the opposition of pagan life and thought. It nurtured personal piety such as finds glorious expression in the Psalter, and it developed a religiously minded judgment regarding the details of life in all its phases which found rich expression in Job, Ecclesiastes, and Proverbs. There were many counter-currents of thought in the Israel of the fourth century or so. The books of Ruth and of Jonah express the protest of some noble souls against the excessive application of the idea of exclusiveness. Judaism did not deaden the popular mind and heart, but stimulated it to joyous, earnest hopefulness. It was a real embodiment of a thousand years of fine religious experience and thinking organized into a system of procedure which aimed to exalt God, to promote holiness, and to prepare for executing His will. It had both the advantages and the dangers of organized truth. The Jewish people were now ready for their historic task.

# XI

## THE TWO AND A HALF CENTURIES OF GREEK AND MACCABEAN RULE IN PALESTINE

### I, II MACCABEES; JOSEPHUS (330–63 B. C.)

Alexander the Great, 336–323

#### PTOLEMIES OF EGYPT

Ptolemy I, Soter, 323–285
Ptolemy II, Philadelphus, 285–247
Ptolemy III, Euergetes, 247–222
Ptolemy IV, Philopator, 222–205
Ptolemy V, Epiphanes, 205–182
Ptolemy VI, VII, 182–146
Egypt annexed by Rome, 30 B. C.

#### SELEUCIDS OF SYRIA

Seleucus I, 312–279
Antiochus I, Soter, 279–261
Antiochus II, Theos, 261–246
Seleucus II, Callinicus, 246–226
Seleucus III, Cerannos, 226–223
Antiochus III, the Great, 223–187
Seleucus IV, Philopator, 187–176
Antiochus IV, Epiphanes, 176–164
Syria annexed by Rome, 63 B. C.

#### HASMONEAN (MACCABEAN) RULERS

Mattathias
Judas Maccabæus, 166–161
Jonathan, 161–142
Simon, 142–135
John Hyrcanus, 135–106
Aristobulus I, 105–104
Alexander Jannæus, 104–78
Alexandra, 78–69
Hyrcanus and Aristobulus, 69–63
The kingdom annexed to Rome, 63

The two hundred and fifty years which followed the substitution of Persia by Greece as the dominant influence in Asia, although unrecorded in any document which is a part of the recognized Old Testament, was of great significance to the Jewish people and to the Judaism through which they gave expression to their views of God and of life as governed by Him. The century or so during which that Judaism had been adjusting itself within and without had resulted in a documented interpretation of Jewish origins and history which made every Jew regard himself as a special child of God, designated to exhibit the obedience and service due from one; in a written law which provided the proper method of such obedience; in glorious traditions which challenged the devotion of every loyal Jew; and in a priestly and scribal leadership which tended to express racial ambitions along religious rather than secular lines. These decades of steady obedience to the Law had not, as the Psalter shows, taken the heart out of religious life. On the contrary, it preserved and fostered that genuine enthusiasm of devotedness which found expression in such psalms as 15, 84, 91, or 119.

Over against this closely organized and efficient Judaism arose a distinctly different world force, Hellenism, sure in time to become antagonistic, since both Judaism and Hellenism aimed at universal recognition. The story of this quarter millennium includes the rise of Hellenism, its influence upon Judaism, the inevitable struggle between them, and the new Judaism which emerged from that struggle, shaped afresh for the New Testament age.

## 1. Alexander the Great and Hellenism.

By Hellenism is meant the spirit of Grecian culture, expressed in Greek institutions, literature, and life, the most powerful agency ever known for the rapid substitution of civilization for barbarism. It was introduced into Asia by Alexander the Great, who, in a few years, not only conquered the Persian empire but all Asia as far as the heart of India. He and his successors settled groups of Greeks everywhere, protecting and favoring them, so that during the third century B. C. little centres of Greek culture spread widely over Asia. The Jews in Palestine not only were within range of the direct influence of such great cities as Alexandria and Antioch, where they were welcomed as citizens and given much freedom of life, but were literally encircled by a group of smaller Greek cities such as Gadara, Pella, Ptolemais, and Joppa. In his own country a Jew of the third and second centuries B. C. heard the Greek language and was familiar with Greek architecture, dress, and customs. In outside cities he learned to speak Greek, to read his own Scriptures in Greek, and to become familiar with Greek thought and literature. The effect of this contact outside of Judea was to produce the liberally minded Jew, entirely faithful to Judaism yet viewing it from fresh view-points. In Judea it produced two classes, the orthodox, "pious" Jew, who shrank from contact with Greek life and became more and more exclusive, and the Jew who adopted Greek ways, wholly forgetful of all except his immediate advantage. So marked was the difference between Judaism's serious, sacrificial standards and Hellenism's brilliant, joyous, artistic self-centredness, that an eventual conflict between them was certain.

### 2. The Century of Ptolemaic Rule over Judea.

At the death of Alexander the Great in 323 B. C., his vast empire, after twenty years of struggle was divided up among those who had been his generals.

Egypt came into the possession of Ptolemy. Western Asia fell to Seleucus. Each coveted the Palestinian states. Eventually Ptolemy was confirmed in their possession and retained it until 198 B. C. It is generally agreed that the apocalyptic visions in Daniel are a survey in various forms of the Persian and Greek periods, the latter being covered in greatest detail in chapter 11.

The Medo-Persian empire. Daniel 8 : 3, 4, 20.
Alexander the Great. 8 : 5–8a; 11 : 3.
His four immediate successors. 8 : 8b; 11 : 4.
From Ptolemy I and Seleucus I to Antiochus Epiphanes. 11 : 5–20.
The campaigns of Antiochus. 11 : 21–30.
His attempt to suppress Judaism. 11 : 31–39.
The prediction of the sudden end of his career. 11 : 40–45.

The Ptolemies were easy-going and tolerant. They paid little attention to dependencies as long as the tribute was promptly paid. The high priest was the responsible head of the Jewish state. This combination of social with religious responsibilities was the secret of many of the evils which developed. The high priesthood became an office which carried with it opportunities for extortion, and unworthy persons either occupied the office or wielded its authority unjustly. This was the starting-point of the gradual divergence between the priestly rulers who were politicians and those citizens whose chief purpose in life was careful obedience to the Law.

The general effect of this century upon Judaism was stimulating. Such apocalyptical outbursts as Joel, Isaiah 24–27, and Zechariah 9–14, which express the attitude of Israel "against the hostile world" and its expectation of Jehovah's interference to protect and advance His people probably belong to this age. Chronicles, Ezra, and Nehemiah were undoubtedly completed not far from 300 B. C. Quite a variety of literature, including additions to the collection of psalms and the exquisite story of Jonah, bore testimony to the vigor and value of Jewish thinking. But its characteristic product during this age was the "wisdom" writings. These were not precisely what we would call philosophy: they were rather the application of religion to life and its needs. The book of Proverbs aimed to instil the social virtues. Ecclesiasticus covered the same theme more elaborately and impressively. Ecclesiastes was a facing of the problems of life as raised by Greek thought and their religious answer. Job, written a century earlier, was a profound treatment of the problem of suffering. Many psalms dealt with the moral order of the universe. The universal answer of these writings to the anomalies and sorrows of life was the goodness and wisdom of the omniscient God. Its realization helped to brace the devout soul in the face of trial.

3. **The Relentless Ambition of the Seleucids.**

About the beginning of the second century (198) Antiochus III of Syria, a famous and able leader, wrested Palestine from the Ptolemies. He then planned to conquer Egypt, but was turned back by the Romans, who saw the danger of permitting him to control its resources. On that day was born a purpose more dangerous to Judaism than even the existence of so many Jews in Judea who were Greeks at heart. Antiochus planned a pan-Hellenic league which should be able to resist or even to overwhelm the Romans. At Thermopylæ in 191 and at Magnesia in 190 he tried conclusions with Rome, was overwhelmingly defeated, was forced to yield to Rome all Asia north of the Taurus range and had to pay 15,000 talents. While plundering a temple to get the money to pay this indemnity he lost his life.

> From Alexander the Great to Antiochus Epiphanes. I Maccabees
> 1 : 1–9.
> Plots of the pro-Grecian renegades. II Maccabees 2 : 1–4 : 6.
> The attempt of Antiochus to abolish Judaism. I Maccabees
> 1 : 10–64; II Maccabees 4 : 7–7 : 42.

His grandson, Antiochus Epiphanes (175–164) inherited this ambition. He, too, was a remarkably capable man, but unscrupulous and erratic. It seemed essential to his purpose that Judea as well as the rest of Asia should "hellenize." He had the aid, not alone of the Jews who were already Greek at heart, but of the high priest, who was his appointee, and, being responsible for the taxes, was taken from the Hellenistic party. So steadfast, however, was the great body of Jews that when Antiochus returned from an invasion of Egypt during which he had been ordered by the representative of the Roman Senate to give up its conquest or take the consequences, he determined in his rage to abolish altogether the stubbornly maintained religion or to wipe out its adherents.

Jerusalem was made a Greek city, held by a garrison. All who refused to submit were dealt with ruthlessly. Circumcision, the keeping of the Sabbath, and the reading of the Scriptures were strictly forbidden. An altar to Olympian Zeus was erected on the site of the altar of burnt offering, and within the sacred precincts a swine's flesh was sacrificed (168 B. C.). The horror of all this to a devout Jew is almost unimaginable.

### 4. The Maccabean Uprising.

It was clear to every one that the very existence of Judaism was at stake. This conviction nerved real

Jews to risk all. They exhibited a heroism unsurpassed in history. The book of Daniel was a priceless source of comfort and encouragement to them by its timely stories of God's support of those who were absolutely loyal to Him in the midst of trials, and by its assurances that the power of Antiochus, however exercised, was destined to cease after a limited time, and that the Kingdom of God would surely be established. The best history of those days is given in the books of First and Second Maccabees.

> The bold resistance of Mattathias and his family. I Maccabees 2 : 1–28.
> The successive victories of Judas, the military leader, over the Greek armies. I Maccabees 2 : 29–4 : 35; II Maccabees 8 : 1–9 : 29.
> The restoration of worship and maintenance of independence. I Maccabees 4 : 36–5 : 68; II Maccabees 10 : 1–8.
> The long struggle for complete independence. I Maccabees 6 : 1–13 : 41; II Maccabees 10–15.
> The reign of Simon. I Maccabees 13 : 42–16 : 24.

The Jews found a leadership in the stalwart family of Mattathias, a priest, of the Jewish family of Hasmon, who openly slew the Syrian commissioner in whose presence he, his family, and the villagers of Modein were ordered to sacrifice to Zeus. All fled to the wilderness and began a warfare, under the leadership of this family, conducted with such skill and energy that within two years four Syrian armies were defeated and the fifth forced to retire to Antioch. Judas Maccabeus, the Jewish general, was now free to enter Jerusalem and to remove every trace of its defilement. In December 165 B. C., with great rejoicing, the regular Jewish temple service was again established.

5. **The Winning of Complete Independence (165-143 B. C.).**

For the next twenty years the future of the Jewish province was uncertain. The Ptolemies of Egypt were very friendly. When the last faithful high priest, Onias IV, was deposed by Antiochus in 170 B. C., he fled to Egypt, where he was welcomed. At Leontopolis the reigning Ptolemy helped him to build a temple like that at Jerusalem, and to found a community which exercised much influence in later history. But the Ptolemies had no political strength. Judea's persistent foe was the ruling king of Syria, whose resources were enormous. Holding their own against him made the Hasmonean (also known as Maccabean) rulers of Judea shrewd diplomats no less than skilful fighters. Judas Maccabeus, who won for his people the boon of religious freedom, was succeeded by his brother Jonathan, who, though having many reverses, took advantage in masterly fashion of disputed successions to the Syrian throne to gain one concession after another, until at last he was recognized as the civil, military, and religious ruler of an enlarged Judea. The one remaining brother, Simon, in many respects the ablest and noblest of all, succeeded Jonathan. Demetrius II of Syria, in return for his support, gave Judea complete independence.

6. **The Maccabean Kingdom (143-63 B. C.).**

The next eighty years were of great importance to Judaism. Josephus relates their events in his "Wars" and "Antiquities." The reign of Simon was on the whole peaceful and prosperous. He refrained from calling himself a king, but was a real sovereign, devoted to the interests of his people. In him the theocratic ideal seemed a reality, so that his grateful subjects proclaimed him high priest and made the office hereditary in the Hasmonean family. John Hyrcanus, his son and successor (135–105 B. C.) considerably enlarged his dominions by conquering and annexing Perea, Samaria, and Idumea. He used the spoil to beautify and strengthen Jerusalem. So great a warrior was manifestly a poor high priest. The strictly minded Pharisees, both many and influential, demanded his resignation of the sacred office. This angered him, made him a supporter of the liberalists, and thus helped to emphasize the religious differences of the day. The next king, Aristobulus, was Greek in sympathy. After a year's reign he was succeeded by a brother, Alexander Jannæus (104–78 B. C.), a despotic, revengeful, vicious man, very offensive as a high priest to the religiously minded of his people. When they exhibited their feeling he ordered a massacre. The Pharisaic partisans revolted but were cruelly put down. He enlarged his dominions and gained some fictitious glory, yet brought on several deplorable results. The most dependable Judeans became hostile to the dynasty; the rivalry between the popular parties became bitter, and the resources of his kingdom were drained. He was succeeded by Alexandra, his wife (78–69), who favored the Pharisees. They misused their influence by oppressing their rivals. Her reign was, however, a "golden" period for Judaism. The synagogue became an elementary school and scribes the teachers of the youth. The yearly Temple tax for Jews everywhere was instituted. All Judaism was drawn together. At her death a civil strife arose between her two sons, Hyrcanus II and Aristobulus II. This dragged on with varying fortune until 63 B. C., when Pompey, the Roman general, solved the dispute as arbiter by annexing the kingdom to Rome.

## 7. Its Importance for Judaism.

These eighty years of Jewish independence witnessed every sort of conduct, noble and treacherous, supremely devoted and totally unreligious, progressive and reactionary. Only for brief periods was there a real union of political and religious wisdom. Nevertheless the period was of great importance to Judaism. It gave Jews everywhere a fresh sense of racial unity. Jerusalem became the one beloved centre and symbol of their religious faith. The boundaries of Jewish influence were greatly enlarged: Jewish culture broadened. The whole Old Testament was probably completed not later than this period. Its translation into Greek was finished. Not a little literature which we know chiefly by name appeared. Judaism expressed itself vigorously.

The most important result of independence was the development of the great parties, the Pharisees and the Sadducees, those who supremely honored the Law and those who were friendly to Greek culture and outside influences. The Pharisees were a religious sect, intent on a scrupulous obedience of the Law, caring for nothing else. Their simple devotedness won them popular influence. The Sadducees grew out of the circle of worldly-minded priests. They held the Temple and its services sacred, but they were aristocratic politicians, believing in worldly-wise policies. Between the two parties developed a bitter antagonism. The scribes, the interpreters and authoritative teachers of the Law, were naturally of Pharisaic sympathies. The great mass of the people had an immense respect for the Pharisees, but no idea of imitating their scrupulousness. The activity of these parties was not affected by the loss of independence.

## 8. The Jewish People (63 A. D.).

When the Hasmonean kingdom ended, the Old Testament era ended also. Under Roman auspices a new age dawned. For a thousand years, ever since the days of David, the Jewish people had been developing a peculiar identity which not only made them a marked race, but also gave them a distinctive influence in history. It remains to sum up what they had become. When Pompey annexed Judea he took over more than a small province with its inhabitants. He assumed political control of a vast religious brotherhood, scattered over the world of his day, linked together by loyalties far keener and deeper than those of dynasty or race. Israel was not a theory but a fact. Jerusalem and its temple were symbols of a religious devotedness that impressed the world by its reality and persistence. Good citizens wherever they lived, the Jews maintained their careful adherence to their own ways in a society of their own. The synagogue, the written law, the other Scriptures, the scribal leadership, wrought them into a religious unity which no other people knew. They had been deprived of nationality, but confirmed in something more permanent. As a nation pure and simple their career was of minor significance; as a factor in bringing the world of the Greek period face to face with true ideas of God, man, and the universe, they had attained supreme significance.

# XII

## A GENERAL SURVEY OF OLD TESTAMENT HISTORY

The popular view of Old Testament history is often colored by a feeling of racial prejudice, or by a yet more potent sense of religious fervor. It is judged to be the record of a great failure nationally, or of a progress so sacred as to be beyond critical inspection. The student of that history may be affected by either attitude, yet realizes that the Hebrew people, whatever their failings, played a recognizable and most important part in the development of the world of to-day. They laid the basis on which Christianity was reared and which furnished two other persistent religious faiths with that which gave them vitality. A survey of the growth which enabled the Hebrews to render this great and unique service is more than a historical advantage: it is a religious experience. The Hebrews staked their all on fidelity to religious ideals. They were pioneers in applying the principles of Divine and human fellowship to every-day life. Their history thrills one with the spirit of idealization and promotes the art of living rightly.

### 1. How Old Testament History Resembles All Other History.

The history of the Hebrew people is a part of the history of the world. It must be judged in fair accordance with established principles of historical criticism.

The Hebrews learned, as all other peoples have done, through experience, both bitter and happy. They were not kept from making serious errors of judgment. They were deeply disappointed over what seemed to be their own failures. Yet they discovered their own genius and gave it play. The Hebrews were not puppets even in the hand of God, but a people which He found useful for His larger purposes.

Viewed as secular history, that of the Hebrew people is not without merit. Despite the fortunes which entirely extinguished other smaller peoples of their age, the Hebrews persisted and discovered a type of life which could flourish. With others the loss of accustomed conditions was the loss of nationalism, and later of identity: the Hebrews made their anticipated misfortunes a cause for readjustments which preserved and heightened their own national genius.

Viewed from the mere standpoint of national greatness, the history of the Hebrews is meagre. As a nation they held a relatively unimportant place. They came to their greatest political strength by reason of the inaction of the greater powers in the world of their day and at the very peak of their prosperity and influence they succumbed to the newly aggressive Assyrian conqueror, knowing no real independence thereafter for six hundred years. Intellectually they borrowed as much as they gave. Yet they were quick and keen in adapting to their own purposes the culture of the nations with which they had contact and in holding a steady progress toward the great goal achieved, one none the less real because it was obscurely approached.

## 2. Its Uniqueness.

The outstanding glory of the Hebrew people is their definite contribution to the clear religious thinking of mankind. In four centuries following the days of Amos, they developed teachings regarding God, humankind, the world, and their right relationships which shape the best thinking of the world of to-day. This teaching gave expression to ideals as well as duties. It reached a climax in the teaching that the highest use of life and power is the sacrificial not the selfish use. It is the justification for regarding them as one of the truly creative peoples of the world to whom it stands forever indebted.

The Hebrews themselves believed that they were God's peculiar people, selected out of all other nations to serve Him and to declare His will. They often overemphasized their exceptional place in God's esteem. However, such a broad-minded man as the author of the book of Jonah rebuked severely such an attitude, showing that God's love is universal. Isaiah 40–55 declared that their entire experience from the days of Abraham had been a Divinely guided course of training which fitted them to declare God's true character and purpose to the world, so that He should stand revealed in His full glory and goodness, and further declared that this witnessing was to be their sacrificial task. Inspired by such leaders, the Hebrew-Jewish people recovered from the collapse of what had been left of their sovereignty and devoted their creative energies to the advancement of the knowledge of God in the world. Whether Judaism was more or less worth while than Prophetism is a matter for discussion. It was, at any rate, an intentional improvement.

The Hebrews not only gave the world a vision of the Divine in life: they supported it by the Scriptures. The Old Testament was a definite means of broad enlightenment, especially after it had been rendered into Greek. Its outstanding quality needed no interpreter, although its range of ideas demanded study. In architecture, in the fine arts, and in the correlated realms of life the Hebrews shared no unusual genius. But in literature and religion they left the world their debtor. The adequate interpretation of God as a moral Being, the exhibit of religion applied to life and the Scriptures were their world-uniting products.

### 3. Its Turning-Points.

The one who reviews the thousand years from Moses to Roman rule recognizes certain dates which serve as turning-points in that gradual growth.

> The entrance into Canaan. About 1150 B. C.
> The disruption of Solomon's kingdom. About 937 B. C.
> The appearance of the Assyrian as a foreign yet overmastering influence in Hebrew life. About 740 B. C.
> The Babylonian exile. 587 B. C.
> The establishment of Judaism. About 400 B. C.

With the entrance into Canaan came a radical change in the conditions which shaped Hebrew life. They exchanged as a people a nomadic, shepherd life for a settled, agricultural life. With the disruption two contending elements in the life of the people, each with its own value, gained greater freedom of expression. The Northern kingdom, however erratic and brief, gave opportunity for the development of what was most creative in Hebrew life. When the predatory Assyrian cast a baleful shadow across Hebrew statesmanship, the real expression of Hebrew genius began. With the exile to Babylonia and elsewhere another radical and permanent change in Jewish fortunes took place. They became essentially a cosmopolitan people, engaged for the most part in business. With the adoption at Jerusalem of the Law as presented by Ezra the scribe, the Jewish people became a congregation or a church.

These five turning-points demarcate the great eras of growth which we must recognize.

## 4. The Significant Eras.

The natural periods of growth under which the student may wisely seek to organize the whole range of Hebrew-Jewish history are indicated in the appendix. The following table aims only to indicate the distinctive eras of development, several of which should be subdivided for purposes of closer study.

> The gradual attainment of nationalization and a sense of competency. Until about 750 B. C.
> The gradual formulation of religion on a moral and spiritual basis. From 750 to about 550 B. C.
> The organization of religion so as to be in complete control of life. 550 to 400 B. C.
> The proclamation of that religion through the dispersion. 400 B. C. onward.

From the days of Moses to the Assyrian age, the Hebrews were becoming a distinctive people, trained through varied experience to understand life. Each one of the five centuries were contributory to this broadening and should be viewed accordingly. For the next two centuries the Assyrian overlordship made their political status stationary. As a people they continued to develop culturally and socially, but their genius expressed itself through the prophets from Amos to Ezekiel and his great contemporary, Jeremiah. The real work of these two centuries was the development of religion on the true and permanent basis which the world has accepted. These centuries represent the Hebrews at their best.

During and following the exile with the continuing political hopelessness a new leadership with a new objective prevailed. The task to which the scribes set themselves was that of organizing religious life completely, so that its ideals should be exactly fulfilled. With this accomplished about 400 B. C., Judaism set itself everywhere to the task of maintaining these ideals and thus was, often unconsciously, the means of proclaiming them abroad.

## 5. Its Leadership.

The Hebrew-Jewish people cannot be fully understood without some comprehension of the organized groups which influenced their social, intellectual, and religious development. Although a strongly democratic people, they accepted royalty with its burdens and values. Some of the kings like David, Jehoshaphat, Jeroboam II, Hezekiah, and Josiah were real leaders, primarily thoughtful for their people and glad to do them good. But the influences which more definitely shaped the popular life came from four groups: the prophets, the priesthood, the scribes, and the wise men.

Greatest of these were the prophets, who interpreted the national life in terms of righteousness and faith, and insisted on worthy ideals in public and private life. They really set the national standards and caused Israel to be an original contributor to the world's good. Only second in importance and far greater in steady influence was the priesthood, which came into prominence and independence along with the prophets and eventually gained entire control of the people. They expressed religion in an orderly programme to be carried out with unceasing care. From their ranks developed the scribes during the exile, who gave themselves to the formulation into specific ordinances of the religious obligations of the individual and of the community.

But the prophet was naturally an idealist; the priest was keen to maintain exact conformity to tradition. The wise men were needed in order that the many-sided applications of religious principles to the practical problems of life might be considered.

The priesthood played a part in the national life as early as the days of David; the prophets rendered their supreme service during the two centuries including the exile; the scribes and wise men became of value with the post-exilic age. Each contributed a real share of the gift of the Hebrews to the world.

## 6. Its Outstanding Personalities.

History gains its perennial interest through those unusual personalities through whose influence the world advances. Such men are few and rare. Hebrew history has its fair share of them from Moses the introducer of that which distinguished the Hebrews from other peoples like them, one of the great figures in history, to Nehemiah, the favorite of Artaxerxes, ready to exchange the life of an influential courtier for the arduous tasks of community reform. David was another great personality, alike in his virtues and failings. He was a man of vision, not, like Solomon, overestimating the real place and power of his people, but forecasting their growth and establishing its sound basis. Elijah was a great original character, who had but one idea, yet it brought the nation back to a sense of its rightful allegiance to God. Hosea, Isaiah, Jeremiah, Ezekiel, and the nameless Isaiah 40–55 had each a creative religious genius which made a contribution to the world's religious thinking. Josiah might have been a great leader in time. The recognition of these in no sense prevents the recognition of the vastly larger number of splendid souls who in less memorable fashion did their duty nobly. Hebrew history abounds in the mention of men and women like Deborah the brave leader, Samuel the shrewd and sane guide of his people,

Jonathan the fine-spirited friend of David, Joab his sturdy and loyal henchman, and very many others who played their respective parts in their own way yet with zeal and courage. The imagination fails to picture the large groups of devoted supporters who, without need of fame, stood together in support of the prophets and the scribes and of other leaders.

## 7. The Literature.

It is evident to a dispassionate student that the Hebrews were in no position to produce literature before David's day. They had records of various sorts, and abundant traditions, but no literary class. From approximately 1000 B. C. on, however, there were those available who had the training and the leisure for literary development. How rapidly it began to appear is a matter of uncertainty. Most of the historical and prophetic literature found in the Old Testament gives evidence of repeated editing, indicating a literary history. The books of Judges, Samuel, and Kings were given their present form in the fifth century or so, but the former began with folk stories five hundred years earlier. The real literary age of the Hebrew people was after the exile, when they laid far greater stress upon literature as a potent means of promoting ideas and programmes. They never ceased to use it freely during the next six hundred years. The last Old Testament historical record is to be dated about 400 B. C. The last bit of writing in the Old Testament may date in the third or second century B. C. The apocryphal books are later still. But outside of all these is the volume of extra-Biblical apocalyptic literature which began to appear with the earliest portion of the book of Enoch in the second century B. C.

The quality of the literature which has been pre-

served in the Old Testament requires no attestation.
It challenges comparison with any other pre-Christian
literature.   As an historical record the books of Samuel
set a standard which eminent historians have recognized.   The book of Job is admittedly a world classic.
The Psalter is the world's hymnal and book of comfort.
The prophetic writings set a standard of spiritual interpretation which no other religious literature reaches.
Those who fail to recognize the lasting merit of the Old
Testament writings are those who have not fitted themselves to have a judgment.

## 8.   Israel's Permanent Contributions to the World.

It is fair to ask, What is the verdict of a competent
historian   concerning   the   Hebrew-Jewish   people?
Viewed in the light of universal history, how do they
rank?   Surely a people whose greatest territory was
no larger than a small North American state, who
maintained their independence only when a great
power was occupied elsewhere, could not stand in the
first rank.   It must be remembered that creativeness
does not go along with size.   The immortal literature
of Greece emanated from a single city-state, during one
short period of free creativeness.

The Hebrew-Jewish people made at least three great
contributions to the world: (1) It developed a sound
scheme of thinking about God, man, the universe, and
their relations, which all sane Christian peoples accept.
(2) It exhibited after the exile a type of religious life
based on principles which impressed the world then
and since and standardized serious life.   (3) It left to
the world in the Old Testament a rich legacy, the value
of which is ever increasing.   Through these contributions alone the Hebrews stand justified as one of the
world's great creative peoples.

# APPENDIX

# I

## OLD TESTAMENT HISTORY BY ITS NATURAL PERIODS

The Old Testament, as viewed by a student, comprises not merely the thirty-nine books included in the Hebrew Bible and in the English Bible, but also fourteen more, known as the Apocrypha, found in the Greek and the Latin versions, and recognized as sacred scripture by the Orthodox Greek Catholic and the Roman Catholic Churches. These added books carry Old Testament history down into the Maccabean age.

The Old Testament records the remarkable growth of the Hebrew people from a stage of extreme social and religious simplicity of life, when it ranked as one of the least important peoples, to a maturity of experience, culture, and religious insight which made it the world's instructor in true religion. The growth thus recorded was alike political, social, cultural, and religious. An appreciation of its stages unlocks the secrets of the Old Testament.

The outline given below seeks to express this growth in natural periods, each one deserving a careful, thorough study by itself and in its relation to the whole sweep of the history and a summarizing of the events, the fine leadership, and the achievements which characterized it.

1. The Beginnings of Human History as Viewed Through Hebrew Racial Traditions (Genesis 1–11).

2. The Gradual Emergence of the Hebrew Clans into History. About 2000–1200 B. C. (Genesis 12–50).

3. The Half Century of Mosaic Leadership and Organization. About 1200–1150 B. C. (Exodus–Deuteronomy *passim*).

4. The Century of the Conquest and Gradual Incorporation of the Canaanites and of the Adoption of Many of Their Religious Habits. About 1150–1050 B. C. (Joshua, Judges).

5. The Century of Rapid Nationalization Establishing Jerusalem as a Political, Cultural, and Religious Centre. 1050–937 B. C. (I, II Samuel; I Kings 1–11).

6. The Century When the Divided Kingdoms Met the Insidious Attack of Phœnician Baalism by a Reaffirmation of Exclusive Loyalty to Jehovah. 937–842 B. C. (I Kings 12–II Kings 10; II Chronicles 10: 1–22: 9).

7. The Century in Which, after Serious Reverses, the Peak of Prosperity and Contented Self-Consciousness Was Reached by Both Israel and Judah. 842–740 B. C. (II Kings 10: 28–15: 7; II Chronicles 22: 10–26: 23).

8. The Half Century of Israel's Collapse and of the Gradual Assyrian Conquest of Judah, with the Reinterpretation by the First Four Prophets of Religion as Essentially Ethical and Spiritual. 740–686 B. C. (II Kings 15–20; II Chronicles 27–32).

9. The Half Century of Unquestioned Assyrian Dominance, with Its Popularization in Judah of Foreign Religious Customs and of an Anti-Prophetic Spirit. 686–639 B. C. (II Kings 21; II Chronicles 33).

10. The Half Century of Religious Reform and Re-organization followed by Rapid National Decline, with the Emphasis by the Second Group of Prophets upon the Spiritual and the Individual Elements in Religion. 639–586 B. C. (II Kings 22–25; II Chronicles 34–36; Jeremiah 37–39).

11. The Half Century of Exile in Babylonia, with Its Social Readjustments, Its Missionary Interpretation of Religion, and Its Emphasis upon Ordered Religious Life. 586–538 B. C.

12. The Building of the Second Temple and Its Re-establishment as Central in Jewish Re-ligious Life. 538–516 B. C. (Ezra 1–6).

13. The Rehabilitation of Jerusalem and Establish-ment of Judaism as the Accepted Institu-tional Scheme of Jewish Religious and Social Life. 516–330 B. C. (Ezra 6–10; Nehemiah).

14. Judaism's Contact with Aggressive Hellenism; Her Inevitable and Finally Successful Strug-gle for Religious and Political Freedom. 330–143 B. C. (I, II Maccabees).

15. The Maccabean Kingdom with Its Inner De-velopment of Judaism, Its Quickening of World-wide Jewish Loyalty, and Its Growing Messianism. 143–63 B. C. (Josephus).

Jewish history did not come to a close with 63 B. C., but the overlordship of Rome which began then should be classified with New Testament history. It will be adequately treated in "Jesus and His Teachings," the third volume in this series.

# II

## GENERAL REFERENCE LITERATURE FOR FURTHER STUDY

This volume has been planned to lay a sound, broad foundation for a life-long study of Old Testament History. It is an introduction to the subject, not a substitute for the more thorough and detailed treatment to be found in a larger history. Its success, in fact, will be gauged by its power to kindle in the mind of the student such an interest in the historical development of the Hebrew people that he will crave a more detailed mastery of many phases of this important and richly rewarding subject. Some of the books which should become known to one who has made use of this volume are hereinafter mentioned. No attempt, however, has been made to append an exhaustive bibliography. The list covers only such reference books as the average student should use. Whoever consults them will find mentioned by them a still wider range of reference literature. Each real student tends to develop his own reference library as he advances in an understanding of the Bible.

Every student of the Old Testament should plan to own, as soon as possible, a good Bible dictionary, a concordance, an atlas, some good commentaries, one or two larger Old Testament histories and a good history of Old Testament literature. The suggestions which follow are intended to assist him in selecting the books which will make a nucleus for his working library.

There are three good Bible dictionaries, each in one volume. The latest and best is Hastings' One Volume Dictionary of the Bible (Scribner's). That by J. D. Davis (any denominational bookstore) is very condensed, but it answers all questions of fact; the other, the Jacobus Standard Bible Dictionary (Funk and Wagnalls), is slightly more conservative in its judgments than Hastings'. There are two concordances which are of handy size, Cruden's and Walker's. The former is sold at a very low price, but is less complete than Walker's Comprehensive Concordance (all religious bookstores). For a large Bible Atlas George Adam Smith's "Atlas of the Historical Geography of the Holy Land" is the best available. It is quite expensive. For all practical purposes MacCoun's Atlas (Revell) is sufficient.

There are three reliable and useful Old Testament Histories in one volume, the author's "History of the Hebrews" (Scribner's) and "Old Testament History," by Professor Ismar J. Peritz (Methodist Book Concern), while George Adam Smith's "Jerusalem," vol. II, is virtually a survey of the history in his fascinating style. Professor Kent's "The Historical Bible," four volumes covering the Old Testament (Scribner's), covers the same ground in much greater detail. On Old Testament literature valuable books to own are Professor Henry T. Fowler's "A History of the Literature of Ancient Israel" (Macmillan), and Professor J. E. McFadyen's "Introduction to the Old Testament" (London, Hodder). For the important prophetical material of the Old Testament the reader may be referred to the second volume of this series, entitled "Old Testament Prophecy" (Scribner's) or to the two volumes on the Prophets in the Messages of the Bible series (Scribner's). A recent and valuable volume which reviews the relation of prophecy to national and world problems is Knudson's "The Prophetic Movement in Israel" (Methodist Book Concern).

Of commentaries there are many. No series is ever of even excellence. Some of its volumes will be far preferable to others. In general it may be said that whenever a student desires a learned, minutely adequate commentary on a Biblical book, he is safe in turning to the International Critical Commentary series (Scribner's). For a reliable yet convenient commentary he may consult one of the volumes of the Cambridge Bible series (University Press). For a terse yet rather satisfying and well-edited help he is generally justified in getting one of the New Century Bible series (Frowde). There are two excellent one-volume commentaries on the whole Bible. Dummelow, "The One Volume Bible Commentary" (Macmillan) is quite useful. Peake's "A Commentary on the Bible" (Nelson) is on the whole the best compact commentary in print. It reflects the historical view-point throughout. Its comprehensive index makes it a real thesaurus of information. Specific volumes relating to particular books or themes will be mentioned below in the references for each study.

# III

## REFERENCE LITERATURE FOR EACH STUDY

The first five references in each section will be to the appropriate pages of Sanders' "History of the Hebrews" (SHH), of Kent's "Historical Bible" (Hist Bib), of Peritz's "Old Testament History" (POTH), of Peake's "A Commentary on the Bible" (P Com), and of Barton's "Religion of Israel" (Bar RI).

INTRODUCTION
  SHH, 3–19; Hist Bib I, 1–3; POTH, 19–40; P Com, 1–17.

CHAPTER I, PRE-MOSAIC BEGINNINGS
  SHH, 23–48; Hist Bib I, 5–150; POTH, 43–63; P Com, 51–57, 63, 82, 83, 133–167; Bar RI, 1–55.

CHAPTER II, FORMATIVE INFLUENCE OF MOSES
  SHH, 49–69; Hist Bib I, 151–229; POTH, 64–95; P Com, 63–64, 84–85, 168–189, 193–194, 196–243 passim; Bar RI, 56–74; Breasted, "History of the Ancient Egyptians," 293–344; "Ancient Times," 80–96, 200; Bible Dictionary, "Covenant," "Moses."

CHAPTER III, GRADUAL NATIONALIZATION
  SHH, 73–119; Hist Bib II, 1–224; POTH, 96–160; P Com, 26–33, 57, 65–67, 85–86, 100, 111–113, 256–300; Bar RI, 75–84; Breasted, "Ancient Times," 200–206; Fowler, "Literature Ancient Israel," 10–65.

CHAPTER IV, THE STRUGGLE WITH PHŒNICIAN
BAALISM

SHH, 125–141; Hist Bib III, 1–50, 112–120; POTH,
163–173; P Com, 58, 67, 73–74, 86–88, 113–114,
300–308; Bar RI, 84–93; Breasted, "Ancient
Times," 206–208; Bible Dictionary, "Baalism,"
"Elijah and Elisha."

CHAPTER V, THE PEAK OF HEBREW GREATNESS

SHH, 141–149; Hist Bib III, 50–52, 121–123; POTH,
173–178; P Com, 58, 69, 74, 308–309; Fowler,
"Literature Ancient Israel," 66–104.

CHAPTER VI, ASSYRIAN AGGRESSION AND PROPHETIC
REINTERPRETATION OF RELIGION

SHH, 149–173; Hist Bib III, 53–111, 123–191;
POTH, 179–203; P Com, 58–59, 69–72, 74, 75,
88–89, 309–311, 426–430; Bar RI, 94–113; Rogers,
"History of Babylonia and Assyria," II, 263–443;
Breasted, "Ancient Times," 208–212; Fowler,
"Literature Ancient Israel," 105–174.

CHAPTER VII, JUDAH'S DECLINE

SHH, 170–203; Hist Bib III, 192–307; POTH, 203–
215; P Com, 60, 72, 73, 89, 90, 312–313; Bar RI,
114–126; Rogers, "History Babylonia and Assyria," II, 443–523; Fowler, "Literature Ancient
Israel," 175–232.

CHAPTER VIII, THE EXILE

SHH, 207–230; Hist Bib IV, 1–34; POTH, 217–245;
P Com, 47, 60, 61, 77, 90–92, 460–470, 501–503;
Bar RI, 127–131; Rogers, "History Babylonia and
Assyria," 523–576; Breasted, "Ancient Times,"
213–220; Fowler, "Literature Ancient Israel," 233–
276.

CHAPTER IX, BUILDING OF THE SECOND TEMPLE
SHH, 231–242; Hist Bib IV, 35–64; POTH, 246–
253; P Com, 61, 78; Bar RI, 131–133; Fowler,
"Literature Ancient Israel," 277–286.

CHAPTER X, THE ESTABLISHMENT OF JUDAISM
SHH, 242–279; Hist Bib IV, 64–145; POTH, 254–
277; P Com, 48, 78–79, 92–94; Bar RI, 133–172;
Fowler, "Literature Ancient Israel," 287–336.

CHAPTER XI, GREEK AND MACCABEAN PERIODS
SHH, 279–308; Hist Bib IV, 146–274, 278–317;
P Com, 48–49, 62, 79–80, 94–97, 271–272, 341–345,
556–558; Bar RI, 173–283; Breasted, "Ancient
Times," 425–451; Riggs, "History of Jewish Peo-
ple: Maccabean and Roman Periods," 1–178;
Fowler, "Literature Ancient Israel," 337–387.

# IV

## QUESTIONS FOR REVIEW

1. What were the organized nations of the Hebrew world when that people crossed the Jordan into Canaan?

2. During the next thousand years what new peoples entered that world and disappeared from it?

3. Why was Palestine so advantageous a home for the growing Hebrew people? When and why did it cease to have special significance for them?

4. What varied factors, racial and religious, had entered into the making of the Hebrew people of the days of Samuel, David, and Solomon?

5. Place in order of importance the six greatest personalities of Hebrew history up to the Disruption in 937 B. C.

6. Prior to the eighth century with its Assyrian dominance what three non-Hebraic peoples exercised the most salutary influence upon the Hebrews, and how did they do it?

7. Samuel is credited (I Samuel 15) with declaring that the Hebrew monarchy would be a social and religious detriment. What was the actual fact?

8. Besides the rulers what other leaders made themselves felt in shaping the national life of the Hebrews? Which group became finally dominant?

9. What various causes led to the breaking apart of Solomon's kingdom? Compare the advantageous with the disastrous results of this disruption.

10. When did Hebrew history in the true sense of the word begin?

11. Trace the story of the growth of the Hebrew national religion through its eight stages as set forth in the Old Testament.

12. In what two senses is "Baalism" used in the Old Testament record? Which was the more dangerous and why?

13. Compare the share of Moses, Samuel, Saul, David, and Solomon in creating Hebrew nationalism.

14. What gave the prophetic order its early pervasive influence and what gave this influence permanence?

15. Name the four great empires which, prior to the days of Rome, counted the Hebrews as a subject people. Which of these exercised the greatest influence upon them and how?

16. What were the marked characteristics of the Hebrews as a people? In what sense is it historically correct to call them a "chosen" people?

17. At what period in the life of the Hebrews did they begin to produce true literature? Why did it appear at that time?

18. What Hebrew king was the greatest statesman of them all? Justify your answer carefully.

19. When did the prophets begin to put their utterances into written form and for what causes?

20. What five personalities—men or women—described in the Old Testament (other than the rulers) impress the student most because of their importance in Hebrew history?

21.  What five personalities seem peculiarly typical as representing Hebrew characteristics?

22.  What five personalities are most helpful to the student through their experiences? In each case give the reason for the judgment.

23.  What kings of Assyria took a direct share in shaping the destinies of the Hebrew people and how?

24.  The Northern kingdom: How long did it last, what two kings shaped its destiny, and what lasting legacies did it leave behind?

25.  What is meant by the Deuteronomic editing of early Old Testament literature? Illustrate by some actual book or passage.

26.  What kings had most to do with the increase in the material wealth of the pre-exilic Hebrews?

27.  When, according to the historians, did the Jerusalem priesthood become influential enough to be able to resist the throne? What influences gave the priesthood final supremacy?

28.  Name five passages in the historical literature of the Old Testament which deserve to be rated as great literature. Justify the choice of each.

29.  How was it that religion among the Hebrews during the last century before the exile both declined and became spiritual?

30.  Discuss the causes which brought about the destruction of Jerusalem and the exile.

31.  Compare the influence on the people of the three great prophetic leaders of the sixth century B. C.

32.  What literary and social renaissance took place during the sixth century, through what class of leaders, creating what religious institutions?

33.  Trace the growth of Jewish sacred law from the days of Moses to the fourth century before Christ.

34. What made the rebuilding of Jerusalem and of the temple of such importance in Jewish life?

35. Of the four great Asiatic sovereigns who ruled the Jews of Palestine after the exile which one best deserves the term "great"?

36. How did the Jews come to be scattered among the nations? In what way was it either a misfortune or a providence?

37. What proportion of the literature of the Old Testament was probably produced after the exile? Name four non-prophetical books unquestionably written later than the sixth century.

38. What gave the Jewish people their remarkable and persistent resiliency as a despised and persecuted people?

39. Compare Judaism with Hellenism. Why could they not be friendly?

40. State the causes, progress, and outcome of the Maccabean struggle. What positive good did it do to the Jews?

41. Who were the two greatest sovereigns of the Maccabean kingdom; what were the causes of its downfall, and the benefits which it brought to Judaism?

42. Assuming three clear turning-points in Hebrew-Jewish history of which the exile was the third, what were the others between 586 and 63 B. C.?

43. Which of the great eras of this long twelve centuries of history seem on the whole the most significant?

44. On which eras should a student of the Old Testament with limited time concentrate?

45. Explain how the Old Testament religion of a Jeremiah and an Isaiah could be the progenitor of both Christianity and of Rabbinic Judaism.

# V

## SUBJECTS FOR RESEARCH AND CLASS DISCUSSION

If this book is used as a text-book by a class, the leader may find it profitable to devote the class session to the discussion of the important themes connected with each chapter. The following list of topics for research and class discussion are suggested as bringing out some of the most essential themes.

### INTRODUCTION AND CHAPTER I

1. The ancient world about 1200 B. C. 2. The racial heritage of the Hebrews. 3. The religious life of the Hebrew tribes before the days of Moses. 4. The historical, religious, and personal values of the book of Genesis. 5. The changes which transform traditions into Scripture.

### CHAPTER II

1. The Pharaoh of the oppression. 2. Evidences from later Hebrew history of the reality of the deliverance from Egypt. 3. The covenant between Jehovah and the Hebrews: its meaning and its historical effect. 4. Changes caused by this covenant in the immediate life of those who came out of Egypt. 5. Moses: his life, character, and place in history.

### CHAPTER III

1. What settlement in Canaan meant to the Hebrew tribes. 2. The changes which two centuries of occupancy wrought in them. 3. The great leaders of these centuries and the specific contribution of each. 4. The development of Hebrew morals and religion from the Jordan to Solomon's temple. 5. The development of a true nationalism.

# APPENDIX 157

## CHAPTER IV

1. The various causes which brought about the disruption. 2. The stamp placed upon Israel by Jeroboam and the resultant differences between the two kingdoms. 3. Baalism, Phœnician and indigenous: its attractiveness and its menace. 4. The prophetic order: its leaders, influence, and service. 5. The six great men of this century who shaped the growth of the kingdoms.

## CHAPTER V

1. The undesirable results of the revolution under Jehu and Elisha. 2. The work of Elisha for his people in contrast with that of Elijah. 3. Aramean peoples of Syria: their origin, location, and the reason for their period of ascendancy. 4. The transformation of the Hebrew kingdoms under Jeroboam II and Uzziah. 5. The social, religious, and political situation about 740 B. C.

## CHAPTER VI

1. Assyria: her rise into dominance and relations with the Hebrew kingdoms. 2. The Northern kingdom: causes of its rapid decline and its contributions to Hebrew nationalism. 3. How the four Hebrew prophets of this century saved Israel from despair and atheism. 4. Ahaz and Hezekiah as statesmen. 5. Hebrew literature: its progress at the end of the eighth century.

## CHAPTER VII

1. The rise of three great kingdoms to rival Assyria and the final dominance of Babylonia. 2. Causes leading to the Deuteronomic revival in Judah and the important outcome. 3. The political decline of Judah and the parallel rise of religious insight. 4. Jeremiah compared with Isaiah as a statesman. 5. Josiah's place in Hebrew history.

## CHAPTER VIII

1. The changes in Hebrew life and thought brought about by the exile. 2. The literature of the Old Testament as produced or revised by the end of the exile. 3. The two great prophetic leaders of the exile and their contributions.

4. Nebuchadrezzar compared with Cyrus. 5. The most momentous change brought about by the exile.

## CHAPTER IX

1. Darius as a statesman. 2. The Jewish Messianic hope as affected by Persian policies. 3. The value of the book of Ezra as history. 4. Palestine as parcelled out in the days of Darius. 5. The significance of the Second Temple to the Jewish race.

## CHAPTER X

1. The old and the new in the Judaism advocated by Ezra. 2. Nehemiah as a typical Jew. 3. The racial significance of a rebuilt and defensible Jerusalem. 4. The Samaritans: origin, claims, and religious history during this period. 5. The literature of the age. 6. Judaism as a religious life.

## CHAPTER XI

1. Alexander the Great: his career, ambitions, and achievements. 2. Reasons for an inevitable conflict between Judaism and Hellenism. 3. What the Maccabean regime did for Judaism and the Jews of the larger world. 4. The literature of the age. 5. Why apocalypse became substituted for prophecy. 6. The two religious tendencies of the Judaism of the second century.

## CHAPTER XII

1. The men who really shaped Hebrew history. 2. The various types of literature to be found in the Old Testament. 3. The Hebrew historical records as compared with other early historical records. 4. The unique elements in the religion of the Hebrews. 5. The permanent place of the Hebrew race in world history.

www.ingramcontent.com/pod-product-compliance
Lightning Source LLC
Chambersburg PA
CBHW021106090426
42738CB00006B/530